I0420411

MODERN
LEADERSHIP
DEVELOPMENT
AND
EXCELLENCE

MODERN LEADERSHIP DEVELOPMENT AND EXCELLENCE

Leadership Excellence

DR.S.K.BABOOA

authorHOUSE®

AuthorHouse™ UK Ltd.
1663 Liberty Drive
Bloomington, IN 47403 USA
www.authorhouse.co.uk
Phone: 0800.197.4150

© 2013 by DR.S.K.BABOOA. All rights reserved.

No part of this book may be reproduced, stored in a retrieval system, or
transmitted by any means without the written permission of the author.

Published by AuthorHouse   05/20/2013

ISBN: 978-1-4817-9522-7 (sc)
ISBN: 978-1-4817-9523-4 (hc)
ISBN: 978-1-4817-9524-1 (e)

Any people depicted in stock imagery provided by Thinkstock are models,
and such images are being used for illustrative purposes only.
Certain stock imagery © Thinkstock.

This book is printed on acid-free paper.

Because of the dynamic nature of the Internet, any web addresses or links contained in
this book may have changed since publication and may no longer be valid. The views
expressed in this work are solely those of the author and do not necessarily reflect the
views of the publisher, and the publisher hereby disclaims any responsibility for them.

CONTENTS

Awaken your real nature, strength will emerge, confidence will emerge, determination will emerge, glory will emerge, purity will emerge, wisdom will emerge, and everything that is excellent will emerge in you once you cast away the veil that is hiding your leadership. This is the highest doctrine of leadership.

Dr.s.k.Babooa.

I have the privilege to hand over this book, to all those who inspire to become the future builders and excellent leaders of their nations. Never stop bringing lights of leadership in the lives of thousand people!

Develop your leadership like a banyan tree under which hundreds of thousands can take shelter and solace. It is useless to know how long you live, but it is worthwhile and essential to know how well you live.

Dr.s.k.Babooa.

PREFACE

You are an exclusive creation of God. You are one without a second. You are unique in your physical and inner beauty. You possess vast and tremendous potential to change the destiny of the world. You are a treasure house of dynamic leadership. **Awaken your real nature, strength will emerge, confidence will emerge, determination will emerge, glory will emerge, purity will emerge, wisdom will emerge, and everything that is excellent will emerge in you once you cast away the veil that is hiding your leadership.**

This book, '*Modern leadership development and excellence*', which you are now holding in your hands, will work magic in your life. You will shine everlastingly like a star on this earth. This is a book of your destiny. I have discovered the gems on leadership development by working with people from all walks of life for over seventeen years. Countless numbers of people have benefited and have seen their lives improved by applying the gems contained in this book.

By lecturing and working with various people, I discovered that a lot of questions were often raised on leadership. I found that many people have a growing interest and inclination on leadership development. Many problems of life are linked with human relationships. Success or failure at home, learning institutions, workplace, public gathering and life in general depends on leadership.

You are a person, who stands out from others, by virtue of your distinctive character. You have a leadership which needs to be polished and developed into an outstanding one. Your leadership is linked with your character which is a building block. In order to make the foundation of your life strong and firm, it is fundamental that you constantly pay attention and devotion to your leadership. **The very root cause of success in your life depends on your leadership. A person is judged by the character he or she possesses. Remember that if you lose money and health, you lose something. But if you lose your character, you lose everything in life.**

I have written this book for you. Hundreds of thousands of people have seen their lives transformed positively by applying the gems contained in this book. So, wake up from your deep slumber. Open the doorway to success in your life by developing your leadership through the gems of this book. I have seen miracles happening to numerous people round the globe through leadership development. An authentic person is judged by the words he or she utters. The physical appearance of a person is at times deceptive. When a person opens his or her mouth to speak, then such a person is judged by others, about the type of person he or she is. The way a person orally communicates reflects his or her real leadership. A picture is often painted of such a person by others. A leadership cannot be shared, bought or sold to other individuals. A leadership is unique to an individual.

During the course of life, a leadership is nurtured and developed. Once a leadership is developed it is imprinted permanently to the individual concerned. Like the first flight of a bird from its nest to the world. Such a bird has confidence in its wings before flying to the realm of the world. Similarly, you should develop confidence in you in order to face the battles of life. Confidence is one of the ingredients of your leadership. This book contains a wealth of gems on leadership development which will enlighten your life, if you apply them devotionally in all your undertakings.

The idea of writing this book came recently when I was awakened in the middle of the night with a feeling to write on leadership development. So, I got up and went straight to my table. I opened my notebook and wrote two words—leadership development. I sat for a few minutes and asked myself. Why at this hour of the night my sleep was suddenly broken? I felt drowsy at that very cold silence night. There was a pin drop silence in my room. After writing the above words, I went to sleep. My eyes opened in the dawn by the melodious tune of the birds. I was still on the bed and looking at the ceiling. I felt ideas emerging in my mind on leadership development. Thus, I again went to write those ideas which cropped up in my mind.

This is how the book came into being. I have written this book to uplift you from misery, failure, difficulty, obstacle, and melancholy. I request you to learn and study this book. The techniques and ingredients given in this book on leadership development will help you grow emotionally, physically, economically and spiritually strong. This book will lead you to peace, happiness, prosperity and wisdom.

'*Modern leadership development and excellence*' will also pull and push you towards success in your life. This book is a product of long and tiring labor. It represents the essence of my research. I deeply thank you for appreciating and reading this book. I am confident that this book will be read and applied by all those who are willing to bring inner transformation. Some of the information in this book has originated from the participants who asked me questions on leadership in my workshops, conferences, seminars and meditation classes. Thus, this book makes you think, reflect, grow and harness your inner power on leadership development.

You will soon learn the chemistry of leadership development and excellence. Hence, this book has been authored for everybody like you who wants to succeed in leadership development and excellence.

ACKNOWLEDGEMENTS

The origin of this book is a result of my efforts and thoughts accomplished following several years of labor. I wish to thank all individuals whom I had met during the highest leadership posts that I had occupied in various workplaces. It was a real laboratory to learn human behavior and interaction. Many people round the world have inspired me on leadership development. It is not possible to name all of them as they are numerous. Nevertheless, I wish to thank everybody who has inspired me directly or indirectly to write this book.

I am certain that this book will continue to play a dynamic role in transforming human leadership into excellence. In the preparation of this book, I am particularly grateful and immensely indebted to the publisher and his enthusiastic team for their marvelous task in bringing this book into its present form. I could foresee the evolution for this book. Thanks to the support of the publisher. I wish also to thank you for reading this book. I extend my thanks to all those who have attended my leadership training courses and seminars. My acknowledgement goes to hundreds of thousands of people who have found this book inspiring and life transforming. **I have the privilege to hand over this book, to all those who inspire to become the future builders and excellent leaders of their nations.**

Never stop bringing lights of leadership in the lives of thousand people!

In accomplishing this noble task, I wish to place on record my sincere thanks to Mrs Pratimah Babooa, Mr Pranav Babooa and Miss Saanvi Babooa for their encouragements. Last, but not the least, my thank goes to Mr Virren Hurrypaul for all his supports. In these days, a good leader has become a rare bird. Good leaders are a source of inspiration, joy and happiness. I would be grateful to receive your views on this book via post or e-mail (skbabooa@ yahoo.com). Thank you.

skbabooa@yahoo.com

1

INTRODUCTION

You are a wonderful and unique creation on this earth. You have all the necessary ingredients enclosed within yourself. To develop your leadership, you have to believe in your potential. This book, *'Modern leadership development and excellence'*, unravels the ingredients of wisdom that are hidden in you. In this introductory chapter, you are introduced the subject matter on leadership development. Leadership in its simplest form relates to the distinctive characters or qualities of an individual. Every individual is distinct from others. No two individuals are exactly, alike. Even twins from the same embryo are not similar. It is important at the very outset to understand that there is no similar person like you in this world. You are the only one dwelling in your body. Your body is an instrument which carries your inner self. Your leadership emerges from your inner self.

The governor of your leadership is your inner self. Your physical appearance manifests the type of leadership you possess. The informational data base of your inner self register all the ingredients of your leadership. Why a person does not know his or her leadership from the very start of his life? Why the manifestation of a leadership takes time? Why many people are successful and others are unsuccessful in their lives?

Is there any answer to the above questions? Yes, there are many answers. The leadership of an individual is beyond the reach of the eyes. It is real and unique in nature. It is enclosed and hidden in every individual. It starts to manifest when knowledge dawns on a person. The leadership of an individual is often veiled with ignorance and illusion. This veil is removed through true knowledge. When you remove impurities and ignorance, you start to glisten like a diamond.

Learn to dig within you and discover the unlimited virtues that you possess. Allow your virtues to pervade through your leadership. Wake up from your deep slumber and fly high in your life. Craft your leadership by removing ignorance and illusion of life. Be yourself and real in outlook. Do not copy others' behaviors or actions. You have an image completely different from others. You stand out, from others, by virtue of your inner beauty. The treasure house of leadership development is within you. Use your treasure house to build up your leadership towards excellence. Never give up, keep on heading on the pathway to leadership development and excellence.

You will be crowned with success when you continue to work hard towards leadership development. It is essential to remember that you are entitled to work only. Never longs for its fruits. Do your duty in a selfless manner. Results of your labor will come at a later stage in your life. It is like sowing a seed in the dark soil. Your duty is to water the seed with love and affection. The seed will ultimately sprout from the darkness into light. In a similar fashion, darkness from your life will disappear and you will glow permanently. Life is not always smooth sailing. There are many ups and downs in life. At times, you may feel like crossing a river infested with crocodiles. Face up the eventualities of life with firm a determination and courage. Thus, your leadership excellence will not manifest overnight, it will take time to do so.

Success or failure depends very much on you. You possess limitless power that can open a whole new horizon in your life. At no point in your life, you should give up. You should always keep the motion of life in action. Action is life and inaction is death. Stop not until you succeed in any undertaking. Life is like a running stream of water. It always moves forward. So, never lament over a past failure. Dwelling in the past is like living with the dead. Let the past be the past. The past is not with you. The future is also not with you. The future cannot be enjoyed today. You do not know what exactly the future will look like. Therefore, in between the past and future lies a gap. This gap is now. You should always live with the present moment. In the present moment, an individual experiences the real treasures of peace and happiness. When your mind is at rest, you will be able to plunge deep into the ocean of leadership. The greatest instrument that you have is your leadership. There are hundreds of thousands of people who have attained success by using the secret of this book in their daily lives. So, it is now your turn to do the same. Learn to tune your leadership towards positive thinking.

Let me give you a brief example of how I change failure into success in my life. Life in my early days was very hard and difficult. I was born in a very poor family. I had to toil and moil in the field with my father and mother. Our very survival depended on soil work. Every day before going to the school and after returning from the school, I had to work in the field. Our family consisted of five children, mother and father. All of us were living at my grandmother's house in one small room. As years went by, my father was able to construct our own house. We had to live from hand to mouth.

My school life was horrible. The teachers neglected me in the class because I was not taking private tuition with them. My father was not in the position to pay for my private tuition. Also, I remember the car accident in which I was involved. It was a Saturday morning while crossing the road near my house; I was swept away by a passing car. I was wounded. I would have been torn to pieces. My life would have finished. But by the grace of God, I was alive. I laid motionless and senseless on the road side. When I opened my eyes, I saw that I was encircled by my father and the bystanders. Following that accident I had to stay at home and I missed the school examinations. I also remember the long stay at the hospital following an infection in my abdomen. All these affected my studies. I started to fall behind in the examinations. I miserably failed the final school examination twice. I was compelled to leave the school. A shadow felt over me. I felt helpless and hopeless. My whole life looked bleak. But my father gave me hope. He said to me: 'do not give up'. He admitted me to a private school. He had to pay for my school fees. We faced financial hardship. Day in and day out, I worked hard both in the field and at the private school. My hard work was answered. Eventually, the final examination results were declared, and I just obtained the minimum pass mark.

From here on, a ray of hope penetrated in the gloomy life of my family. I continued to study hard and started to obtain very good marks in the examinations. I even came first in a subject in my country. I started winning gold medals in sports and excellent grade in the examinations. My dream was to pursue university education, but alas! My father passed away. When this happened, my life became extremely hard. I had to ration food and clothing. I waited for a very long period of time before getting a job. After joining the hospital as a student nurse, I continued to study through distance education. Working day and night, I saved each coin to finance my studies. I had to work and study at the same time. Studying alone for university courses was not easy. I had also to look after and support my younger brother and sister.

Later, I got married and constructed my own house. I continued to study by taking loans. I received constant and continuous support from my wife for higher studies. Both of us studied altogether. Another tragedy of life that snatched the happiness from my face was the sudden death of my younger sister. Her death was a severe blow to my life. Despite this, I did not give up. Today I am a PhD holder. I am completing another PhD degree. I have three master's degree, two bachelors degree and six diplomas. I have occupied top leadership position in various institutions. I have never studied in the campus of a university, but I have been the top administrative leader, University Registrar.

I failed examination many times in my early life, but later I became the chief examination officer in the university. I have undergone the ups and downs of life while shouldering higher responsibilities. All this became possible with the support of my wife. Life is a battle field. We have to struggle to survive. Perseverance, tolerance, endurance and determination are some of personal qualities that are required to face the battle of life. I have changed failure into success. I started my life from the scratch. Continue to develop your leadership. Call upon your sleeping higher consciousness and see how it rises up to glow your leadership.

This book gives you the necessary knowledge for opening the locked doors of your leadership. It uses simple techniques and down-to-earth approaches to leadership development. I have discovered these gems in men and women from all walks of life. The unique characteristics of this book will appeal to you.

In chapter 1, the author, Dr S.K.Babooa presents his life experiences of changing failure into success. The meaning of leadership is given in chapter 2. Chapter 3 focuses on the dormant power of your mind. It gives a detailed explanation on the working of your mind. It also provides a practical approach to deal with the problems of life. Chapter 4 analyses the importance of positive attitude on leadership development. Chapter 5 deals with faith as an important constituent of leadership. You will come across self-confidence in chapter 6. It gives you practical information on self-confidence. Chapter 7 discusses fearlessness as an essential component of your leadership. You will find in this chapter a practical guide line and advice on how to remove fear in the process of leadership development Chapter 8 focuses attention on courage as well as a practical guide line on how to develop courage. Self-determination is an important ingredient of leadership development. This is discussed in chapter 9. Chapter 10 presents a detailed explanation on serenity. In this chapter, you are given practical advices and guides on how to remove worry, stress and tension. These hurdles upset serenity. Chapter 11 devotes attention on self-sacrifice as an essential aspect of leadership development.

Detachment is another important component of leadership development. This is discussed in chapter 12. Chapter 13 highlights the importance of self-commitment on leadership development. In chapter 14, self-discipline is discussed in detail. Chapter 15 presents self-patience as an important aspect of leadership development. Righteousness helps you to develop your leadership. This is discussed in chapter 16. Chapter 17 concentrates on character building. This is followed by a discussion on positive manner development in chapter 18. Chapter 19 discusses honesty as the life blood of leadership development.

Humility is a fundamental component of leadership development. You will find a detailed discussion of humility in chapter 20. Chapter 21 focuses attention on compassion as an essential component of leadership development. In chapter 22, you will learn on self-control as an instrument to leadership development. Chapter 23 emphases self-motive as a driving force on leadership development. The power of forgiveness is discussed, in greater detail, in chapter 24. Acceptance is another important component of leadership development. This is explained in chapter 24.

Responsibility is another important ingredient of leadership development and this is presented in chapter 26.

Further, chapter 27 discusses the power of concentration in the process of leadership development. Self-knowledge is an essential constituent of leadership development and this is explained in chapter 28. Enthusiasm cannot be overlooked in leadership development. Hence, chapter 29 discusses the importance of enthusiasm.

Similarly, chapter 30 presents personality as a vital component of leadership development. Leadership discussion is incomplete without referring to vision. So, this is done in chapter 31. Moreover, you will find in chapter 32 an analysis of imagination as a key ingredient of leadership. A leader needs to have an ambition and this is discussed in chapter 33. Chapter 34 illustrates how to deal with failure in leadership development process. A leader very often has to face criticism and this is discussed in chapter 34. Emotions are part and parcel of leadership development. In chapter 36 you will find a detailed explanation on emotions. Chapter 37 devotes attention on the importance of tolerance in leadership development. Last, but not least, chapter 38 discusses the importance of persistence on leadership development. This book closes the topic on, *'Modern leadership development and excellence'* with a conclusion.

2

WHAT IS LEADERSHIP?

At the very outset of this fascinating subject on leadership development and excellence, it is vital to understand, what leadership entails.

Leadership comes from the word lead. To lead is to cause someone to go with one by way of guidance. Leading is linked with direction and guidance. A leader is a person who leads. Leaders are either good or bad. A good leader, directs, guides and leads whereas a bad leader misdirects, misguides and misleads. Generally, a leader uses autocratic, democratic, laissez-faire and bureaucratic styles of leadership. In pursuing his or her goals, an autocratic leader acts in a conformist way using rigidity and tolerance. A democratic leader encourages participation of his or her subordinates and followers. Likewise, a laissez-faire leader exercises very little or no authority and leaves everything in the hands of his or her subordinates and followers to accomplish their goals. However, a bureaucratic leader exercises power by commanding subordinates to follow relatively inflexible rules. Usually, a leader is formal or informal. A formal leader occupies a specific position in the hierarchy of an organization or institution. Similarly, an informal leader does not necessarily occupy a formal position, but derive his or her leadership by way of influencing others.

Leadership, therefore, is the process of influencing the behaviors of subordinates or followers in such a way that the goals set by the leaders are realized. Leadership covers the entire spectrum of human aspects such as intellectual, social, economic, political, behavioral, physical, spiritual, psychological, biological and environmental.

Leadership is an essential modifier of human behavior. This book provides the knowledge for changing and training individuals into good leaders.

A good leader possesses features such as insight, sound health, skills, maturity, integrity, diligence, compassion, dedication, devotion and good character. These are some of the building blocks of leadership. Your positive thoughts are the architects for building your character. Your capacity and potential will move you towards success, but your character will always keep you successful. A good character reflects value such as humility, loyalty, discipline, courage, honesty, responsibility and sacrifice. A leader who possesses a good character remains unaffected like a steady rock in the wind. A leader who does not possess a good character is like a pot full of holes, incapable of storing divine nectar of human elements. So, keep your character good and strong by applying the knowledge contained in this book.

A good leader thrives and blossoms like a lotus flower even in the muddy environment. Such a leader sends perfume of sandalwood although grown near a poisonous tree. He transforms hundreds of thousands of ordinary individuals into a leader of good character.

Remember that the destiny of your country rests on the characters possessed by your leaders. Also, a good action of a leader at times, speaks louder than his or her words. So, learn to perform good actions and leave behind your noble foot prints on the sands of time like the great leaders of the world. As you will go through the pages of this book, you will sense your inner power of wisdom and your zeal to empower your leadership.

3

LEADERSHIP AND THE DORMENT POWER OF YOUR MIND

Your mind is the greatest asset for developing your leadership. Your mind possesses unlimited power. The dormant power of your mind needs to be harnessed and awakened. Understanding the mind is vital for developing leadership. Your mind is found in your brain. Your brain and mind is not the same thing. Your brain can be compared to the hardware part of your body. It is divided into two hemispheres. The hemispheres are further divided into various lobes. As far as your mind is concerned, it is considered as the software part of your body. At this stage, it is essential to understand that your body, mind and spirit are different entities. All these fashion your leadership. Your brain is responsible for processing the instructions that are received from your mind.

Your mind has a memory which is called the informational data base. Your memory can be short-term, long-term or subconscious. Usually a short-term memory remains for a few seconds or minutes. Your long-term memory functions for a long period of time. As regard to the subconscious memory, it carries original and eternal impressions of the past. It possesses unbound and dormant energy. Many people recall their previous births. Impressions, from a previous life come from the subtle body that is the spirit. Both your spirit and subconscious mind influence your leadership. Your spirit is eternal, original and everlasting. Your spirit is birth less and deathless. Your spirit is beyond the reach of your eyes. It never dies when the body ceases to function. It moves from life to life until liberation. Your spirit, therefore, functions in close relation with your subconscious mind.

Your spirit is enclosed in five coverings. These coverings have different functions. The first one manifests joy, happiness and bliss. The second covering represents the 'aura'. The 'aura' is a protective covering around the body. It can be seen by a person who is clairvoyant. Clairvoyance is the ability to feel, sense and see images which an ordinary person cannot. The third covering is your physical body which carries various functions such as respiration, movement, reproduction, nutrition, growth, excretion and irritability. The fourth covering of your spirit is concerned with intellect and emotion. The fifth covering represents the mind. Your mind is divided into conscious and subconscious mind. Your conscious mind functions according to the desires, rules, wishes and regulations of your body. On the other hand, your subconscious mind operates in accordance with the will of your spirit. Thus, there is a constant interaction between your conscious and subconscious mind. Mental conflicts occur due to interference of impulses from the conscious and subconscious mind. All this has an impact on the leadership development of an individual.

The conscious mind uses only a very small part of the total mind for daily activities. Once its task is accomplished, the conscious mind is withdrawn from that task. It then moves to another task. So, this cycle continues. The conscious mind is also the source of negative emotions such as fear, depression, arrogance and hatred. It is often entangled in confusion and conflict.

As far as the subconscious mind is concerned, it is highly powerful. It is with you all the times. Your breathing rate, heartbeat, vision and cellular functions are under the responsibility of your subconscious mind. Your subconscious mind occupies the largest part of the total mind. It is a source of unlimited, original, creative and dormant energy. All these have a direct bearing on your leadership development. One of the ways to enter the subconscious mind is through meditation. You will find in this book how meditation plays a key role in opening the door of the subconscious mind. Your leadership will shine once you have activated the dormant energy of your subconscious mind. Thus, any darkness in your pathway to leadership development will vanish.

Your mind, therefore, is a fertile soil in which thoughts keep on germinating like weeds. Every second a thought takes birth and dies. Not all thoughts are positive. Some thoughts bring joys, happiness and peace. Other thoughts bring pains and sorrows. A close inner observation will reveal that you are a bundle of thoughts. A thought, therefore, has an impact on your leadership. Positive thoughts help to develop a strong leadership. Understanding the phenomenon of thoughts germination in your mind is important to develop your leadership. Selecting a particular thought requires a strong inner discipline. I have come across many people who have no control over their thoughts. They run after their thoughts without having any control on them. When this happened they feel exhausted, depressed and restless. All these reflect distinctly on their leadership. Remember that in any crop growing field, the weeds grow faster than the edible crop. If nothing is done, the weeds eventually invade the edible crop. Similarly, you should not allow negative thoughts to crop up in your mind. All actions in life start with a thought. If the thought is positive, then the action is also positive. An action has its power to generate its own fruit. If you do a good action following a positive thought, you will be garlanded with good fruits. Therefore, there is no power on this planet earth which can prevent an action from reaping its fruits, whether sweet or sour.

Action is life and inaction is total doom. Your action in life is responsible for your leadership development. An action is like a flowing stream of water. Likewise, your leadership shines following a good action.

In order to better understand the philosophy of thoughts and actions, it is fundamental to empower your mind. Your mind becomes highly powerful in complete silence and peace. Thoughts are obstacles to harness mental power. In silence, you will have a perfect control over your mind. Your mind needs to be fixed and absorb in your inner self. The dormant power of your mind will emerge to shape your leadership.

One of the ways to accumulate inner power is to sit daily in silence. Bring inner silence in you. Just observe your thoughts. Do not follow them. Learn to grow and move from a thought stage to a non thought stage. The gap between two thoughts needs to be extended. You will learn more about this on the section, meditation. The subconscious mind is opened in deep silence. This tool is the gateway to success in your leadership development endeavor.

One of the greatest secrets to leadership development is the power of positive thinking. You should have a perfect control of your mind so that your level of concentration becomes high and powerful. A controlled mind is beyond pain and pleasure. It is a purified one. Such a mind detaches itself from all attachments. Remember that attachment brings pain and suffering. The bitter reality is that nothing physical in this world is yours. Even your body is not permanently yours. You will have to leave your body one day. So, learn to live a neutral life. Learn to respect and do a good action for the interest of everybody. Always concentrate on your action. Do not attach with your action. Do the action for the sake of action. Love all, but hates none. This will liberate you from the bondage of your mind. Always keep a firm control over your actions. I have seen many individuals who complaints day in and day out about failure in their lives. They are unable to control their thoughts. Consequently, they feel miserable and moves aimlessly with their frustrated minds.

You should learn to deal with any problem related to your leadership in the quickest possible way. Never leave a problem to linger for a long period of time. Your mind is the most powerful tool to deal with any problem on leadership.

You have read in the introduction of this book some of the problems which I encountered in my life. In this chapter, I wish to tell you how I used the power of my mind to deal with the problems.

I used a simple technique which worked wonders in my life. I wish to share it with you. In my early life, I was surrounded by the problems of poverty, health, accident and drop out in the examinations. I was completely crushed and disappointed when I failed the examination twice. A moment in my life brought my spirit down and desperate. I felt helpless and lonely in this world. I was drastically neglected and criticized by teachers and laughed by friends. Sitting alone in an isolated beach, I watched the sea waves moving to and fro against an old leafless tree. From that tree, I gained a valuable lesson of life which boosted my mind. I saw in that old, dry and leafless tree the determination to face the ups and downs of life. Although it was an old tree yet it was firmly fighting to survive in its hostile surrounding. I felt that I also have to fight like that old tree. Life is a battle field. I have to fight in order to come out victorious. I analyzed the problems that stand on my way.

I came to know that every problem comes with the seeds of solution. It is useless to keep taking about a problem. It is rather important to use the mental energy to tackle a problem. I came up with the following discovery of the mind.

Reduce the size of any problem into pieces. Use your imagination and think positively on the problem that you wish to deal with. Remember that a problem is usually an event of the past or yet to happen in the future. You should not dwell in the past or future event. In the present moment, no problem troubles us. That is in the present moment you are free from any problem of life. When you start to think and invite a past problem then you experience negative mental emotions. Also, do not worry unnecessarily about a problem that has not occurred. Do not dwell in any future problem which is not within your reach.

Your subconscious mind is very powerful to tackle any problem of your life. Answers to any problem come at the moment you are dealing with them. So, do not waste your mental energy in advance by thinking a past or future problem. Just leave any problem in the hands of your subconscious mind. Tell your subconscious mind to find a solution to your problem. In the meantime, just watch like a spectator on the problem from a distant. Do not attach with any problem of your life. Leave your problem in the hands of your subconscious mind and continue to live your life. Wherever you go do not recall your problem time and again. If anybody raises your problem to its surface, do not react. Just listen to the person and do not jump to a conclusion right away on your problem. Be alert all the times. You will meet many people who come to inflate a problem instead of deflating it. Some people just show sympathy to your problem without any contribution to solve the problem. Wherever possible avoid such people. Enjoy your life all the times by living with the present moment. The present is extremely powerful. In the present, nothing troubles us.

By observing your problem from a distant, you will open your subconscious mind which is your greatest asset. Always believe in you. Do not waste your time with any useless 'ifs' or 'buts'. Move straight to write your problem on a piece of paper or on your note book. Here, you should be careful when writing your problem on the paper. Do not be carried away by your emotions. You should work like a surgeon on an operating table. When dissecting your problem do not attach at all with it. Remember that all problems come with a seed of solution like every dark cloud has a silver lining attached to it. When you cut your problem into small size, you in fact, increase the surface area to volume ratio of your problem. Suppose you have to fry a potato. If you take a large whole potato and put it in the frying pan, it will take a lot of time to fry. The same potato when cut into small pieces and then put in the frying pan will fry faster. In the same way, cut your problem into small pieces. Do not inflate your problem like a balloon. Instead, remove the air of the balloon, it will reduce in size. Never fight or complain about a problem. Instead, go straight to deal with it.

Sit alone in a tranquil place. Accept yourself as you are at this stage in life. Be true to yourself. Look deep within yourself. Knowledge is the power which is hidden in you. Take care not to be moved by any emotion. Discover your hidden power. Your subconscious mind will release the magic gift and dissolve your problem. Your first step in this endeavor must be strong and firm. Write the problem, you are facing on a piece of paper. List the problem in detail. List all the horrible things that occurred to you on the paper. You may experience negative emotions emerging in you. But, be careful not to attach with them at all. You continue to write the problem in detail, point by point. By doing so, you have cut the problem into small size.

Next, you write a heading like how to tackle each of them. Under this heading, list all the possible ways to attack the points which you have listed. Then use another heading like how you want to deal with each of the point listed. In this section, write the way you want to attack and dissolve the problem. By doing so, always keep your problem away from you. Discover your power hidden in you. Discover how resourceful you are. Learn to stand independently in your life. You have come alone to this world and you will depart alone. Stand and die in your own strength. Never and never give up in life. Honor yourself. Know for certain that you are someone very special and real. Value yourself all the times. Know that you are a treasure house of power and worthy of everything in life.

Realize your own identity, power, courage, confidence and determination to deal with any problem of life. Know for certain that any problem contains the seed of solution which only you can discover. Listen to the advice of people regarding your problem. But at the end of the day, only you have to deal with your own problem. Never be scared with any problem of life. Past problems of life should not be awakened in the present. Let the past problems of your life be in the past. Live fully with your present moment. You will realize that time is very powerful. Your subconscious mind governs the time. Time is always on its wings. Time, tide and wind do not wait an individual for long.

So, live your life with the present. Waste not your energy thinking about the past or future problems. A problem of life helps you to develop your leadership. You will realize that your life has meaning and objectives. You are a perfect being capable of dealing with the problems of your life. Never run away from the problems of your life. Always face them with a bitter smile. You will realize that each time you go through a problem of your life; you feel that you have grown up. Remember that going through each problem, you get a new experience. An experience is the best teacher in life. Thus, always go deep within yourself and discover the treasure that you possess.

You are worthy, powerful, resourceful and excellent in everything in life. Value yourself. When dealing with a problem always seek help from your higher Being. Your higher Being is your guide. In the course of life, you receive answers to the problem from different sources. Anyone close or distant at times comes to help you directly or indirectly. So, be receptive and attentive to the message or information. A word from a telephone call can be your instrument to deal with your problem. Divine counsel is heard in deep silence. Thus, learn to receive the direct or indirect counsel from your higher Being.

Your mind should always be fixed on and absorbed in the self. Keep your inner eyes open while engaging in your daily routine activities. To understand this better, let me give you an example. The eyes of a mother bird hatching her eggs remain wide open. Her eyes have an aimless look yet her mind is totally fixed on her eggs. In the same way, your problem when left in the hands of your subconscious mind is under process of finding solutions. Do not worry unnecessarily about your problem. Let your subconscious mind do its work. Do not interfere with your subconscious using your conscious activity. Thus, engage in your various activities while keeping your mind fixed on the divine within you.

4

LEADERSHIP
AND POSITIVE ATTITUDE

————◀o▶————

One of the ingredients of leadership development and excellence is the power of positive attitude. Your attitude is your mental make-up which has a direct impact on all your actions. An attitude relates to thinking and behavioral expression. A positive attitude will garland you with success in life.

One early morning in late July this year, I was sitting alone in my courtyard, when a person whom I have often seen him passing through the road nearby came to see me. He approached me with a worried look. He directly asked me, 'What has happened to your problem'? He also said that he had heard from people and read in the newspaper about a lot of problems I was facing regarding my job. He asked me, 'Are you okay'? I raised my head slowly and with a smile replied him; yes I am happy and fine. He sympathized with me about my problems which he had heard and read in the newspaper. My answer to his question was 'I am currently thankful and grateful for all my problems.' I felt that I had grown stronger while going through all my problems. Further, I replied him that all my problems came with the seeds of solutions. So, they have helped me to find solutions to the problems.

My approach was a positive mental attitude towards the problems. Whatever you do in life is linked with your attitude. A positive attitude changes something impossible into possible. Your positive attitude has a bearing on your work, family, result, performance and country. Your attitude is linked with the quality of your thought. An uncontrolled thought will make you stressed and worried. It is important to put a brake on your negative thought. A positive thought creates a positive attitude which leads to peace of mind. Your positive attitude is manifested through your leadership. Therefore, it is important to develop a positive attitude towards all your undertakings. Honor and respect yourself. Whenever a problem arises, do not react to it. Many people start to panic or become upset when they encounter a problem. Never invite such reactions in your life. Think and do not react to any problem that stands on your way. With a peaceful mind observe the problem. This attitude to problem solving is essential for success. Your mind does not function fully and clearly when it is obstructed with negative emotions. When your mind is free from negative emotions, it starts to produce factual and rational thoughts which solve many problems. Therefore, let your mind do its part in attacking the problems of your life. Always move ahead with a discipline and positive attitude. Your mind, once stimulated and left with your problems, starts to process them.

Your leadership cannot be divorced from your attitude. Attitude brings negative and positive responses. If you stimulate your mind towards negativity then your mind processes negative results. For example, if a person says, 'He will fail and not succeed'. The mind of such person will process this negative attitude. On the other hand, if a person constantly repeats that he will succeed, then the subconscious mind processes this positive attitude. Thus, do not waste your energy complaining about any problem. Just take a positive attitude by planting the seed of positive thought in your mind. Whenever you are dealing with a problem, always concentrate on the problem itself rather than on people who created it. Do not attack people, but attack the problem itself by the method given in the previous chapter. You may have seen people attacking people instead of the problem itself. Keep your negative emotions under perfect control. Do not react openly. Keep cool and alert all the times. Your leadership will start to shine with your positive attitude. You will be attracted like a magnet in all situations. You will be welcomed wherever you go with your positive attitude. Your positive attitude is your strong weapon to protect you against problems of life. Make a solemn desire and nurture positive attitude towards your life. See how wonders will pour in your life. People will listen to you, if and only if your attitude is positive.

Always start your day with a positive attitude. Develop a positive outlook, purpose and goal of your life. Cast off negative attitude. Think positively and develop good faith. The next chapter deals with faith which is another gem of your leadership.

5

LEADERSHIP AND FAITH

Faith is an important component of your leadership development. People will believe in you if you possess faith. Faith relates to complete trust and commitment. You have to remove any doubt that obstructs your pathway towards leadership development and excellence. Faith is also linked with confidence. This will be explained in another section of this book. Firm belief will lead you towards leadership development and excellence. Positive thought is closely related with faith. A positive vibration from your subconscious mind leads to the development of faith. Positive vibration of thought when mixed with faith enables you to change negative emotion into a positive emotion.

Repeatedly, give orders to your subconscious mind. The orders you give depend on your belief. If a person repeatedly says, 'I will not succeed or I will fail'. The subconscious mind of such a person will pick up the instructions received and will process the same. It is essential to note that a faith is developed according to the quality of impulses processed by the subconscious mind. If you develop a firm repetitive positive thought for succeeding in any undertaking, then you will be crowned with success. Good faith is developed, therefore, in accordance with positive thoughts and emotions.

Any step taken with a good faith in life opens a new horizon. Your leadership will glisten when you have cultivated the seed of faith in you. Your subconscious mind has a great power that can go beyond your imagination. A firm conviction and faith will enable you to understand the mysteries of human existence. The door of your spirit will be opened when you use the key of the subconscious mind with faith. Faith will cross all boundaries of your life. Faith is the greatest truth of your leadership.

If you look at the seed of an oak tree, you will perceive nothing special at first. If you break the seed in order to know what is there in the seed. You will see only the physical structure of the seed. If you have faith, your vision will expand as regard the seed. In the seed, a life is hidden—a huge oak tree. This seed reveals its hidden knowledge and power when grown into an oak tree. In your body, there is a spirit that is minute. It cannot be seen with your naked eyes. It cannot be learned by reading books, intellect or physical knowledge of your body. It is revealed to those people who have a good faith. It is also experienced by people who have given up evil conduct. Like the oak seed, everything that your mind may imagine is hidden in your spirit. It is the vehicle of your life. Your body is the dwelling place of your spirit. This tiny spirit is connected with the universe. Your spirit is closely linked with your subconscious mind. To better experience this, it is vital that you possess faith in your ability. Use your faith to go within your spirit through meditation. In this journey, nobody will accompany you. Your spirit will be your only guide in this pathway.

In order to develop faith, eliminate doubts and negative emotions. Learn to cultivate power by introspection and inner voyage through meditation. Your leadership needs faith. Your mental state is revealed through faith. Real faith is the enemy to failure. Therefore, persistently use positive thoughts, in all your dealings in life. Sit in silence for at least 30 minutes every day to cultivate your inner power. Continuously send positive vibrations to your subconscious mind. This will magnetize your faith with positive emotions. Always be yourself. Do not copy behaviors of others. Honor and respect your inner power. Eliminate jealousy, selfishness, hatred or any negative belief on other people. Last, but not the least, develops self-confidence. In the next chapter, you will learn the gems of self-confidence in building dynamic leadership.

6

LEADERSHIP AND SELF-CONFIDENCE

———◀◦▶———

Self-confidence is the magic behind your leadership development and excellence. Self-confidence is the interior feeling of certainty and trust. Self-confidence is your inner force of life. People will believe in you, if you have confidence in whatever you do and say. You will always be surrounded by people, if you possess self-confidence.

My early life was full of thorns. At every step, I had to struggle hard in life as illustrated in the introductory chapter of this book. If you think yourself weak, you will become weak. This is the truth. When I failed my examinations and removed from the school, I did not give up. I took the failure to be a stepping stone to success. I developed a strong inner confidence. Self-confidence can be developed only by you. I have never physically attended any university campus for my higher studies. I had a lot of personal and financial difficulties during my early life. I have never studied with a lecturer in any university. I struggled alone with my university courses for more than twelve years. At every step in my education, I had studied alone and absolutely alone. Handling personal, familial, work and educational challenges become possible only by having self-confidence. My life has been spent discovering the power of self-confidence.

You can develop self-confidence by continuously sending positive vibrations to your subconscious mind. This will trigger positive impulses. Your attitude, belief and faith, will be magnetized. You will feel a new power emerging in you. This power will remove all doubts and negative emotions from you. This power is your inner confidence. Self-confidence cannot be seen with your eyes, but it manifests in your physical body. Self-confidence is not about feeling that you are superior to others. Self-confidence is not also letting others down. Self-confidence is the ability to generate strong inner willpower to face any situation in life. By facing difficulties and obstacles, you become strong. This further boosts your self-confidence. If you have self-confidence, then impossible will melt to possible. Self-confidence will make you worthy and capable of winning the heart of everybody you come across in your life.

Self-confidence can be developed in a number of ways. Each individual has his own way to develop self-confidence. I wish to give in this section some of the ways which I have personally applied in my life.

- Ask and constantly demand your subconscious mind to move you towards the objectives of your life.

- Handover all your problems to the subconscious mind.

- Concentrate on your positive thoughts every day for at least 30 minutes.

- Create a positive faith and belief in you.

- Persistently send positive vibrations to the subconscious mind by accepting yourself as you are.

- Ask your higher Being for power to face any situation in life.

- Saturate your subconscious mind with positive thoughts such as good habits, exercise, prayer and devotion.

- Never criticize people and yourself.

- Whenever a problem crops up, do not panic or feel worried.

- Analyze and deal with a problem as explained in the chapter, the dormant power of your mind.

- Commit to your memory that you believe in you and will never give up until you have attained the objectives set by you.

- Eliminate negative attitude towards life.

- Repeat at least once a day, God is with you all the times to protect and love you.

The above advices will help you to develop self-confidence. Remember that the subconscious mind processes the impulses. It then sends vibrations to leadership development. Impressions from your subconscious are registered in your spirit. Therefore, always honor, accept and love yourself. You will see amazing results in your life.

7

LEADERSHIP AND FEARLESSNESS

Fearlessness is an important ingredient of leadership development. The moment fear envelops you, you are doomed. Fear is the most dangerous enemy to leadership development. Fear is a negative feeling caused by exposure to unpleasant environmental conditions. There are many forms of fears, for example, fear of failure, rejection, death, attack, separation, loss of health, darkness, criticism, raid, insult and so on. Fear in whatever its form, brings down self-confidence, self-esteem, faith and strength of a leader.

If you do not fear anything in your life, then you will do excellent work. Fear is one of the greatest and deadliest enemies of human beings. Remove fear from your life and see how powerful you are. Fear paralyses your thought and makes failure possible. You feel weak when fear clouds your mind. Weakness is a great sin which is triggered by fear. On the pathway to leadership development, if you fear criticism by other people, you will not go ahead. Fear of criticism snatches your smile, your individuality and power of thought.

I remember one day, my neighbor saw me going to my office by bus. He approached me and said people will criticize you if you go to attend duty by bus instead of using your car. I simply greeted him and did not reply. In the back of my mind, I knew that I will learn more and more when mixing with different people. This will help me to learn their behavior, attitude and manner in society. If I had feared of criticism by people, I would not have come up with a wealth of knowledge regarding human characters and behaviors. I always believe that the society is an open laboratory to experiment and learn human behaviors and characters. Always be yourself and know yourself. Do not fear to be criticized by people, stick firmly to your goal in life.

Fear is often expressed as nervousness, awkward behavior, poor body posture, looking away while communicating, poor voice, lack of confidence, laziness and inability in decision making. All these have a direct impact on leadership development. If you want to become fearless in developing your leadership, follow these advices.

- Know for certain that fear is removable. Most fears are baseless and hollow.

- Develop strength, self-confidence and courage to face any fear that comes your way.

- Determine to cast out any fear from your mind. Nurture courage by positive thoughts.

- On a piece of paper, note down a list of things that you fear.

- Do not attach to any fear. Do something to remove your fear.

- Work on one fear by dissecting it into tiny pieces. So, discover the origin of your fear. You will find a lot of reasons for your own fear.

- Never inflate any fear by exaggerating its size, always cut the fear into small workable form.

- Your list must be completed honestly and carefully.

- Now analyze and study your list. Make another list, the ways how to attack and solve them. Remember not to have the least attachment with your fear.

- Develop inner power by constantly meditating on your inner self. Your subconscious mind will release the antidote to your fear. Believe in your higher Being who is your protector and torch bearer of light on your pathway. All darkness of fear will vanish when your subconscious mind will come into play.

- Keep a positive attitude towards your thought. All your actions must be done disinterestedly. Do your duty for the sake of duty. Leave the fruits of your labor in the hands of your higher Being.

- Increase the flow of your faith into your subconscious mind. Saturate your subconscious mind with fearless approach to life. Commit to deal with any fear by strong determination of your memory and will power. Remove your fear of people and physical world.

- Remind yourself time and again that you are more powerful than any baseless fear. Imagine yourself to be always free from all fears.

- Always face things that make your afraid of. Do not be afraid of anything in life. You will do wonderful and marvelous progress in your leadership development.

- Never associate or identify yourself with any fear. Observe fears from a distance like a spectator. It will come and depart without touching you if your inner force is strong.

- Fear is usually something of the past or future. At the present moment, it is inexistent. Therefore, do not dwell in the past or future fear. Live your life fearlessly in the present. Never invite any past or future fear in the present moment.

- Have a strong trust and faith in your ability when dealing with any situation in your life.

- Always visualize your success, peace and happiness in life. Project positive vibrations in all the environments you enter. At no moment let fear approach or touch you.

- Take everything positively that nature has built for you.

- Do not react to any fear. Simply remain distant from it.

- Do not feel inferior in the presence of others. You have the same potential and capacity like anybody on this earth. Just develop them by strong determination and see what wonder you can do in your life.

Throughout my life, I have used the above to deal with any fear. Awake, rise high up and cease not, till you attain success. Transform and change your life towards fearlessness.

Turn any fear of failure into positive strength. Remember that strength is life and fear is death. In the next chapter, you will learn how courage can overcome fear.

8

LEADERSHIP AND COURAGE

Courage is an essential human quality needed for leadership development. Life is not always a bed of roses. There are also thorns in life. Remember, courage will keep you moving through the tribulation of your life. There is no individual in this world, who has not undergone pains or sufferings. Courage is the ability to face life bravely. Life on this earth demands a great sacrifice. You need to be courageous, in order to face the battle of life. If you want to develop your leadership towards excellence then cultivates courage.

Your courage will give you conviction to feel, believe and act bravely. I remember the day when I visited a holy place in Varanasi during an international conference. There was a great hustle and bustle at the place. I passed through the holy place. There were many monkeys roaming on the ground. They shrieked, all of a sudden, they started to approach me. When I turned my back, they became more aggressive and started to annoy me. I felt to be torn away to pieces. An old man who was sitting nearby, shouted in a loud voice, 'Do not be afraid and just face them'. I instinctively picked up his advice and courageously faced the monkeys. When I stopped and looked into the eyes of the monkeys they started to run away from me. **From that day, I learned a precious lesson. By facing trouble courageously, we attain victory. Remember cowards always lose in life. You will attain victory in life through courage. Your faith, belief and courage, will stand you firm in all situations in your life.**

Always fight fears and troubles when they come your way. The Mount Everest was conquered by Edmund Hillary through constant courage. He had to try many times before he conquered the Mount Everest. Christopher Columbus discovered America through his courage while going round the globe. Another great example is Charles Schwab who built the United States Steel Corporation with conviction and courage. There are many examples of people who have come out victorious in life by their courage. The electric bulb was invented by Edison. Penicillin was discovered by Fleming and John Logie Baird failed many times before inventing television.

Courage can be developed by consistent effort. Anything that is great in life starts initially from small. An idea can be small at first, but when developed courageously can bring wonder in life. Always remember that successful people have started with small and grown big through their courage.

- Develop your inner power by constantly stimulating your subconscious mind. All inventions and discoveries have originated from the subconscious mind of people.

- Accept honestly if you have failed in any task. Then go step by step to tackle your task, keep fear of failure under control. Abraham Lincoln failed many times in the elections in America before he was crowned with success. Nelson Mandela had to go through many failures before succeeding in abolishing apartheid in South Africa. Similarly, Mahatma Gandhi had to face failure many times before bringing freedom to India. Maurice Chevalier, being a great entertainer, lost his job because of mental health problem. A series of failures started to come in his professional life. He lost faith and self-confidence. Later, with courage he overturned his failure into success by accepting honestly his fear. He acted courageously by removing all his fears of failure.

- Any great achievement goes through hindrances, hurdles and obstructions. You have to be prepared to face them with courage. A flag rises and floats always against the wind. Similarly, if you want a special achievement, you need to have a greater courage when failure comes. By constantly keeping courage to its surface, you will prevent negative thought and negative attitude from emerging.

- Pay serious attention to your mental potential. Your subconscious mind will process positive thoughts. Always think boldly, fearlessly and act firmly in order to generate courage.

- Develop courage by thinking that no failure is everlasting.

- Always concentrate to do a duty, in the right way instead of the wrong way.

- Courage is developed by constantly remanding yourself how to do a work efficiently and effectively.

- Keep any failure away from you. Never admit any failure. Saturate your subconscious mind with positive thoughts.

- Work diligently towards your goal.

- Ask your higher Being to give you direction and power in order to face any situation in life.

Therefore, courage eliminates all types of fear. **Your life will become a smooth sailing boat in the rough ocean, if you develop courage. It is not by escaping or running away from troubles that lead to success. But by boldly confronting them, you will attain victory**. Thus, courage will inspire you to excel your leadership.

9

LEADERSHIP AND SELF-DETERMINATION

Self-determination is one of the most essential components of leadership. You may have many objectives in your life. To accomplish them, you need to have self-determination. No one can work for your objectives. It is only you have to work towards your own objectives. Remember that apart from the objectives you have set in your life, your life itself has a major purpose on this earth. Your highest goal is liberation or emancipation. To attain any purpose of your life, you need self-determination. You must have full faith and belief in you. Self-determination requires firmness in your decision making capacity. Decide precisely what you want to achieve and set the goal accordingly. Once you have taken a firm decision stick to it until you attain it. No matter what happens, keeps your decision making power alive all the times.

When I set my goals from failure to success in my early life, I encountered a lot of discouragements from people. At no point in time, I listened to those who brought hurdles on my pathway to success. I was determined to succeed at all costs in my life. To pass my final examination was my first goal. I worked day in and day out alone. My positive thoughts were my companion on the pathway to the examination. Eventually, I was garlanded with success in my examination. In the same way, I proceeded to other objectives of my life.

Many people fail in their lives because they lack self-determination. **There is nobody who can decide for you.** Your friend, relative or anybody can help and advice you in decision making. But at the end of the day, it is you who will take the decision. Any consequence of your decision will have to be borne by you. Learn to stand on your own feet all the times. **Living a life full of dependency on others weakened your own ability and decision making power. The secret to success in leadership development lies in self-determination. The first flight of an early bird from its nest is a determined one. You have to stand firmly like the bird standing at its nest from the tree top to start its first flight in the world. You must have faith, trust and confidence in your inner ability. The bird that makes its first flight has faith, trust and confidence on its wings. It may encounter difficulties at first to have equilibrium in the air, but with self-determination, all obstacles vanish.**

Self-determination helped Henry Ford to wheel people in beautiful cars. The life of Henry Ford is an excellent example of self-determination. He possessed an outstanding leadership. This brought him to world recognition. William Henry Gates (Bill Gates) and Arnold Schwarzenegger are living examples of self-determination. Bruce Lee, William

Burrough, George Mendel, Alexander Fleming and Martin Klaproth are examples of persons who possessed self-determination in their lives. There are boundless examples of achievements of people in various walks of life. All achievements are linked with self-determination. You have a strong weapon to inculcate self-determination that is your subconscious mind. In your decision making, use your subconscious mind. It will positively help you to take a firm decision. You may encounter a lot of influences from other people's opinions. Their views or opinions will have little or no impact on your leadership ability. Too many opinions of the people will have little value in your life. An opinion which is realistic and workable is highly valued in life. Its success depends on a leader's ability and determination to put it into operation.

Your journey in life depends very much on your self-determination. Setting your plan and the goal is not enough. **You have to constantly water the seed of your plan and the goal with love, affection, devotion and determination. Once determination has taken its firm root in you, you will fly high in your life. Nothing will come to trouble or worry you from moving ahead.** Self-determination teaches you the value of self-help. I have learned to depend on myself.

At every stage of my life, I have stood alone to face the battles of life. You may have come across people who have helped you in a certain situation. It is always good to receive help, but a help should not become a dependency for eternity in life. Learn to help yourself. **Self-help is the best help in life**. Depending too much on people reduces your self-determination power. **Your own power is triggered** by your inner Being. Always keep your subconscious mind on alert. You will grow into a determined master of your destiny. It is not by escaping from, but by facing a problem we become strong. Develop your self-determination and see the miracles that you can bring to the world.

You are a special gift on this earth. Focus on your self-determination ability and bring out your image through your leadership.

10

LEADERSHIP AND SERENITY

Serenity is a fundamental aspect of leadership development. Your physical outlook operates according to the nature of your subconscious mind. Your physical appearance is manifested as a result of the internal state. Serenity relates to the inner tranquility and calmness. If you suffer from the inner turmoil like worry, tension and stress, then you will find it very difficult to cope with any situation in life. All these are generated from your mind. If you leave them to propagate, then your whole leadership will be serious upset. Serenity leads to peacefulness. Until and unless your mind is serene and peaceful in extremely demanding situation, you will success in leadership development.

There are many people who try to show off and copy the behaviors of others. In doing so, such people lose their true nature and creative ability. Always respect and know yourself. Accept your inner core and potential. Admit all the times that you are strong and powerful. When I say be yourself, I do not mean that you feel superior to others. Do not develop any arrogance. This is a negative attribute. Also, do not feel that you are inferior to others. Being yourself means that you need to think positively about your strength and inner capability. Honor, value and respect your inner self. You are not unique only, but a special being.

Let me now give you some advices on how to deal with inner turmoil. One of the obstacles to serenity is worry. A worry is a disturbed state of mind. It gives an uneasy feeling. A worried person dwells on constant troubles. A worry usually originates as a result of doubt or lack of confidence. If a worry is not removed then it changes into a fear.

- A worry is removable. Do not attach to any worry.

- Write the thing that is worrying you, on a piece of paper. List all the factors that have generated the worry.

- List all the possible ways to deal with the worry. Then select the appropriate alternative.

- Remember not to attach with any worry. Leave the worry in the hands of your subconscious mind.

- Never leave a worry unattended. Always seek help from your higher Being. Saturate your mind with positive thoughts.

- Remember that a worry is a thing of the past or future. At the present moment, do not invite it. Many people worry unnecessarily about things that have already occurred or yet to occur. So, shake off the foolish waste of your mental power.

- Generate inner power by dwelling in constant inner silence and peace.

- Develop full faith and confidence. Your positive approach and attitude will uproot any worry that stands on your way to progress.

- Never allow any worry to enter your mind. Always fill your subconscious mind with positive thoughts such as power, courage, peace and fearlessness.

- A worry is a negative emotion. Thus, saturate your subconscious mind with positive emotions.

- Know for certain that your higher Being is with you all the times. Thus, there is no question to worry unnecessarily on anything in life. You are always protected by your higher Being in absolute peace and silence.

In order to attain serenity, you need to be tension free. A tension is a mental strain that blocks clear and positive thinking. A person who is tense never attains serenity. To remove tension you need to breathe deeply. Observe the movement of your breathe. By deep breathing, you increase the oxygen supply to your brain. By doing so, your mind gets stimulated.

- Sit in silence for at least 30 minutes every day. Empty your mind by extending the length between the two thoughts. Read the chapter on concentration in this book.

- Do gentle walk or physical exercise based on your health state.

- Imagine that you are the most powerful than any negative emotion.

- Cultivate peace and silence within yourself by meditation.

- Fill your mind with positive thoughts. By doing so, tension will leave your mind. Repeat daily the breathing exercise. Serenity will prevail all the times.

A stress is an obstacle to serenity. A stress is a negative pressure on the mind. When you are in great stress, your mind is blocked. If a stress is not removed, it changes to burn out. This is a state of physical and emotional exhaustion. In order to remove a stress, you should know its source.

- The seed of stress will germinate if you continuously water it. Therefore, deprives a stress from its water supply.

- Not only cut the root of a stress, but uproot it completely from your mind. Remain detach with any stress.

- Cultivate positive thoughts in your subconscious mind. Have trust and confidence in your ability.

- Develop a habit to sit in silence so that your attention is drawn on your breathe. Breathe deeply in and out through your nostril. By doing so, your mind will detach itself from your body and will connect with your inner self. Then tranquility and peace will submerge you.

- Leave your stress in the hands of your subconscious mind. Let it dissolves your stress.

- Develop positive attitude towards people around you. Do not criticize or blame anybody.

- Visualize that you are highly powerful than any stress.

- Develop self-confidence, self-determination and courage in all your undertakings.

- Always take full responsibility of all your undertakings.

- Imagine that at the present moment, you are completely free from stress. A stress is a matter of the past or future. Do not invite or dwell with any stress.

Therefore, serenity is upset as a result of negative emotions such as worry, tension or stress. Your leadership will glow if you remain in serene in all situations. **Once serenity has** taken a firm root in you, you will be able to go through any hustle or bustle of life without being affected. Thus, take a daily bath in serenity in order to protect and empower yourself. This will enable you to face any turmoil of life will a smile on your lips.

11

LEADERSHIP
AND SELF-SACRIFICE

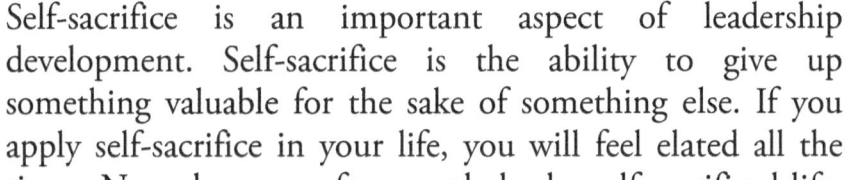

Self-sacrifice is an important aspect of leadership development. Self-sacrifice is the ability to give up something valuable for the sake of something else. If you apply self-sacrifice in your life, you will feel elated all the times. Nowadays, very few people lead a self-sacrificed life. Your mother or father or both of them must have sacrificed a lot for you to lead a happy and contented life.

In any family, the mother and/ or the father work hard to provide shelter, support and solace to their children. They expect that when they will grow old, weak and unhealthy, their children will look after them. Similarly, a mother bird makes self-sacrifice to hatch her eggs and grow the young ones with devotion. **A life which is worthy for others, is an authentic life. If you look at a large banyan tree, you will understand the value of self-sacrifice. The life of such a tree is full of self-sacrifice. The whole life of the tree is spent for the sake of the world. It undergoes hardship of rain, snow, wind, dew and heat in order to** protect others. People take shelter, rest and solace under such a tree. The life of such a tree has a great value for living entities such as insects, birds, animals and human beings. The tree gives everything that it possesses to the world such as leaves, fruits, shade, timber, flowers, roots, bark, wood and ashes.

You are a part and parcel of nature. You depend to a certain extent on others and others depend on you. There is a harmonious balance and equilibrium between you and the environment you live. The give and take philosophy is linked with self-sacrifice. Your life on this earth becomes meaningful when your energy, power and intelligence are used for the betterment of one and all.

There are many people who live just for themselves. They lead a selfish and greedy life. Such people never go far in life. They confine themselves within the four walls of their houses like prisoners. By doing so, they develop a negative attitude towards others. Remember that a human being is a gregarious creature; he or she cannot dwell in isolation. We need company, interaction, and give and take through self-sacrifice. **Develop your leadership like a banyan tree under which hundreds of thousands can take shelter and solace. It is useless to know how long you live, but it is worthwhile and essential to know how well you live.**

12

LEADERSHIP
AND DETACHMENT

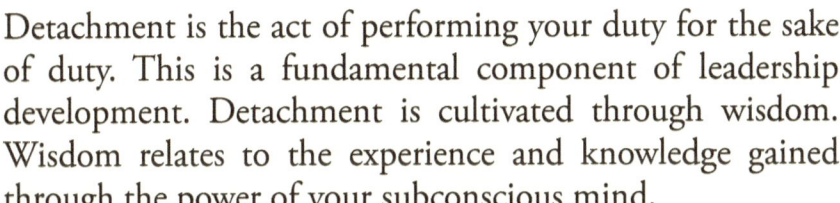

Detachment is the act of performing your duty for the sake of duty. This is a fundamental component of leadership development. Detachment is cultivated through wisdom. Wisdom relates to the experience and knowledge gained through the power of your subconscious mind.

Your life is full of actions. **An action is like a running stream of water. Action is life and inaction is death. You cannot escape from the fruits of your action. Good action brings good result and bad action yields bad result.** The state of your mind is linked with the duty you perform. If you do your duty well, then you get not only peace of mind, but also good result. **You are entitled to your duty only. The result of your duty is not within your reach.** The outcome or result of your duty is not in your hands. You cannot get a result now while performing your duty in the present moment. You have to wait patiently. **If you sow the seeds of rice today, you cannot get the rice immediately. Also, if you sow the seeds of**

thorn instead of the seeds of rice then you cannot expect rice for the harvest. Once you have performed a duty, you should detach from it. It is unwise to spend energy on the future outcomes of your duty. If you open the ground daily which contains a seed it will die. Therefore, your duty is to water the seed with love and devotion. The seed will sprout when the time will come. If you attach yourself with your duty, you will experience pains and sufferings. **Doing duty for the sake of duty brings peace of mind**. Once you have performed a duty, detach from it. This will free your mind.

Detachment does not mean that you do not care for others. Taking care of a person is a duty. What detachment teaches is that you do your duty for the sake of duty and not for the sake of reward. You have a control over your duty, but you do not have a control over the results of your duty. The law of nature says that any attachment to the physical world leads to suffering. Anything that is precious to you when it is lost brings pains. **Your body is a vehicle in which you dwell temporarily. Your higher spirit, mind and body, are separate entities. If you analyze deeply, you will realize that even attachment with your body, brings suffering. Therefore, adopt the philosophy of detachment in the performance of your duty. You will cross over your life without being drowned. You will reach perfection. Your deed and action will purify your mind. You will rise like a glistening star in the world.**

13

LEADERSHIP AND SELF-COMMITMENT

Your life becomes meaningful, worthwhile and purposeful when you are self-committed. Self-commitment is an important part of leadership development. It is a commitment set by you, to attain your goals in life. Self-commitment is a determining power to move boldly and consistently towards a goal. If you are self-committed, then your life becomes a smooth sailing boat in the rough ocean. Nothing will scare you. Self-commitment is also a trust that you place on your ability and capacity. Self-commitment will always keep you moving ahead in life.

I have had to struggle consistently in my early life. It is the commitment which I set in my life that has brought me out of obstacles and difficulties. Self-commitment will move out any block from your pathway. It is a magic power that is harnessed through the subconscious mind. Use your subconscious mind to generate consistently your inner power of commitment. Do not give up at any moment; continue to forge ahead towards your goal. Self-commitment will work wonders in your life. A bird constructs its nest with small dry leaves little by little. Every moment, every day, every week, every month or every year builds your life with commitment. Self commitment will enable you to develop faith, determination and a strong sense of responsibility. When you have developed these, you will overcome obstacles and hurdles of your life. Self-commitment will also enable you to have patience, endurance, tolerance and perseverance. There are many examples of people in the world who have attained success through self-commitment. Florence Nightingale revolutionized the nursing profession through self-commitment. Margaret Elizabeth helped hundreds of thousands of sick by self-commitment. Mother Teresa worked relentlessly to help the sick and needy people. She did so by her self-commitment approach. Doctor Albert Schweitzer is another example of noble person who served and treated hundreds of sick in Africa. The world is full of examples of self-committed individuals. Remember your strength and power lie in your self-commitment. Thus, you can overturn impossible into possible by self-commitment. Therefore, awake, get up and take your first step in leadership development through self-commitment. You will move ahead in your life with self-commitment.

14

LEADERSHIP AND SELF-DISCIPLINE

Self-discipline is another important ingredient of leadership development. Self-discipline will enable you to move towards your goals in life. Self-discipline is your guiding light. You have to keep this light always burning. The darkness from your pathway will vanish. Self-discipline is concerned with refining of character, behavior and self-control. All these become possible once you have opened the gate of your subconscious mind. Self-discipline is not punishment. It is not harming or underestimating others' potential. Self-discipline is the ability to distinguish between a good and bad action. Sowing the seed of self-discipline in your life requires self-commitment.

The world and universe have been created in a perfect order. It is bounded by knowledge. The knowledge of the world and the universe is revealed to those people who are self-disciplined. The scientists work in a disciplined way, unraveled hidden knowledge of the world. The discoveries and inventions are products of a disciplined mind. Nature has built its own discipline, a harmonious balance between the biotic and a biotic world(living and non-living things).

Self-discipline will fine tune your subconscious mind. Your interior environment is regulated by self-discipline. Self-discipline originates from higher knowledge, which manifests in your behavior. In order to generate self-discipline, learn to turn your eyes inward. That is to sit in silence and observe your breathe. In silence, your subconscious mind sends positive vibrations. This will help you to produce self-control over your life. Always look at your life with positive eyes. Value your life with honor and dignity.

A life without self-discipline is like a ship sailing in the mighty rough ocean without a rudder. It moves aimlessly in the ocean with the wind. On the other hand, a life which is self-disciplined moves courageously in the vast rough ocean with a proposed destination. Such a life arrives at its destination, safe and sound that is liberation.

Success in a house is not achieved by its physical infrastructure, but by the discipline prevailing among the family members. Discipline makes a strong bond among family members. **Similarly, your body is not only like a house, but a temple. Keep the kindle of light burning through self-discipline, your life will glow with victory.**

15

LEADERSHIP AND SELF-PATIENCE

Self-patience is part and parcel of leadership development. The result of your labor does not come up overnight. It takes time. Self-patience relates to a calm endurance to hardship. It is the ability to have a self-possessed waiting potential and capacity. Wherever you go, you will see that people are always impatient to get immediate results of their works. Self-patience judges your ability to remain in self-control in the unstable situation. Self-patience has a life's duration. It starts from the time you perform an action until the result is obtained. It requires looking into the future. As explained in this book, if you spend your energy in the future then you will develop negative emotions. If you are carried away by negative emotions then your mind is blocked.

There are many people who do not possess the ability to keep their patience under control. If you are on the way to a long distance by a bus, do not worry unnecessary when the bus will reach its destination. Wait for the time; you will arrive at your destination. Just enjoy your travel. Similarly, if you take the case of a student who embarks on a four year degree course, he or she has to wait for this duration before completing his or her course. This requires self-patience.

In the course of this four year degree, the student needs to enjoy each moment of his or her life. Time never waits for anybody. Time is like a running stream, it goes in the forward direction. At the end of this period when the degree certificate is handed over to the student, the student realizes that most of the joys of student life have gone. Remember that the real joy is not in the reward you receive, but it is in the precious moment when you are fulfilling your duty. Therefore, do not be like the poor traveler who lament about this destination, enjoy the journey of your life without worrying about the result. Leave the results in the hands of your higher Being.

Self-patience will do a lot of wonders in your life. Do not force any work to release its reward prematurely. Wait with patience, the fruits of your labor. Do not follow the footpath of the poor gardener who plants different seeds today and goes to pluck flowers tomorrow. Self-patience is required during the whole process of germination till flowering. It takes time for the results to be out. Success in your life will come until and unless you work hard and have self-patience. Do all your duties with devotion and leave the results to your higher Being. Cultivate the seed of self-patience by turning your gaze inward. By doing so, your subconscious mind will germinate the seeds of tranquility and calmness. Let the tiny seed in the soil grow into the future tree. Everybody in this world has to wait for a result. So, keep calm and detach yourself from your duty. Have self-patience in the leadership development effort!

16

LEADERSHIP AND RIGHTEOUSNESS

———◀O▶———

Righteousness is an important aspect of leadership development. Righteous relates to the noble qualities of a person. It is concerned with the virtuous and law-abiding in the performance of your duty. Your good conduct is linked with righteousness. Any act performed with evil motive leads to unrighteousness. Righteousness is cultivated by performing good action. A righteous person leads a life of self-sacrifice, self-discipline, self-commitment and detachment. These concepts have already been discussed in this book.

One of the purposes of life on earth is to lead a life of righteousness. Always do your duty with devotion, respect and honesty. By doing so, you attend purity of mind. Negative thoughts will never trouble you. Negative thoughts like jealousy, arrogance and hatred should not be allowed to germinate in your mind. Your act of righteousness originates from your subconscious mind. Empower your subconscious mind with positive thoughts. **Respect the** rules and regulations of your life. Honor and cherish yourself. Pay tribute to all human beings. All individuals are connected with one another.

Like any individual, you too possess a self. All your actions are registered in your inner self. A righteous action enlivens your inner self. Nobody in this world is immortal.

Therefore, do all your actions with dedication and in the right way. **A human being is distinguished from another human being not only by his or her physical attribute, but also by righteousness.**

Righteousness is, therefore, the observation of a person's duty. It is of no value if you just know righteousness. Applying righteousness in your day to day duty is most important. This is the highest doctrine of leadership.

17

LEADERSHIP AND CHARACTER

Your character is the nucleus of your leadership. A character is the building block of human leadership. It is a collection of mental and moral features. Success or failure in your life is linked with your character. Nurture your character daily in order to shape your leadership and this will help you to attain an outstanding result in your endeavor. Your character is the real picture of yourself. It is your strength and power to face life.

Your character is your inner core that only you know well. Your character is reflected on your behavior. The subconscious mind is your governor of your character. Having a strong and dynamic character will enable you to pass through any troublesome situation in life. Remember that your character can make you good or bad. A good character brings joy and happiness in life whereas a bad character brings pain and suffering.

The core theme of your leadership is your character. **Take a daily duty to visit your character. Uproot any weed that** may have cropped up in the garden of your leadership. You have to water your good traits and value yourself. Character cannot be bought or sold. It is only cultivated by oneself.

Character building requires a continuous process throughout your life. You have to re-visit, re-shape, re-engineer and re-vamp your character daily. Know for certain that it is your character that will stand you in the ups and downs of your life. If a character is left unattended for long, it starts to accumulate impurities which block your subconscious mind. When this happens your leadership is clouded with a veil. By removing this veil, your leadership will start to glow again.

Learn to perform your duty with politeness, kindness, patience, humility and justice. In order to develop your character you must apply self-discipline in your life. Avoid getting tempted to negative influences. Follow righteousness in all your actions. Develop your character by increasing your knowledge of life. Move consistently and positively towards building your character instead of reputation. People will respect you if you are a leader of character. Such leader goes through the turmoil of life by remaining intact.

Have faith and trust in yourself. Do your duty without arrogance, dishonesty and ego. Your leadership will shine.

18

LEADERSHIP
AND POSITIVE MANNER

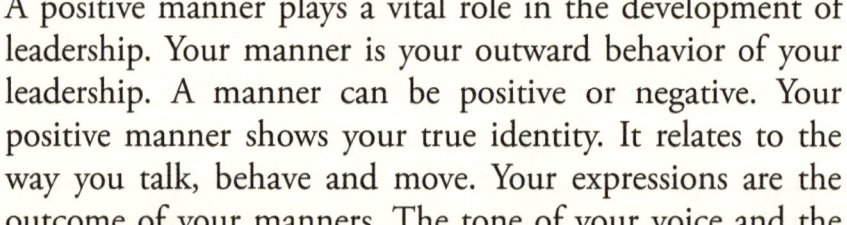

A positive manner plays a vital role in the development of leadership. Your manner is your outward behavior of your leadership. A manner can be positive or negative. Your positive manner shows your true identity. It relates to the way you talk, behave and move. Your expressions are the outcome of your manners. The tone of your voice and the word used by you represent the manner that you possess. People listening you, form their own opinions on the manner you possess.

A positive manner requires a respected command of voice. Your speech must express self-dignity, self-esteem and truth. It also expresses your mental state such as joy, happiness and confidence. A negative manner is expressed by impolite voice and words. Develop positive manners by regularly checking the words you use in communication. Respect and greet people by using the right words. Develop a sound physique, standing and outlook when communicating with people. Your spoken words are the life blood of your communication. Great leaders such as Abraham Lincoln, Mahatma Gandhi and Confucins have been immortalized because of their inspirational speeches. In order to project his good image, Abraham Lincoln, being very poor, borrowed money to buy his clothes when he was elected the President of America.

Do not criticize anyone openly. If you have to deal with a problem which a person is facing then concentrate and attack the problem instead of the person. There are many people who criticize unnecessarily and attack the person who is involved in a difficult situation.

Great leaders such as Albert Einstein, Martin Luther King and Henry David Thoreau attained immortal fame because of their positive manners. Greatness of leaders develops owing to virtuous deeds and manners. To develop positive manners, you need to have a good character. **Your manner represents your conduct. It is the product of your loyalty. Use appropriate words, courtesy, etiquette and body language when talking with people. Speak calmly, softly and confidently with people. Avoid mannerism, falsehood, violence, hatred, injustice and impoliteness.**

You are the only one responsible for developing your positive manners. You are also the teacher and judge of your manners. Positive manners take time to develop. If you look in a field, you will notice that the weeds grow faster than the vegetable. In the same way, people pick up bad manners quickly than good manners. In order to have a positive manner, you need to make a lot

of self-sacrifice. Day-in and day-out, you have to take care of your voice, character, word and body language. A positive manner is a key to success in life. It is like a glowing light which removes all darkness from your life!

19

LEADERSHIP AND HONESTY

Honesty is the life blood of leadership development. People will believe in you when you exhibit honesty in your approach to them. Your deeds and actions must be honest. If you are honest, you will develop self-commitment, self-discipline, self-confidence and positive character. Honesty is truthfulness. Truth is the greatest reality in life. It is like a light which cannot be concealed. Honesty relates to fairness in all your undertakings. You should never cheat, give false and untruthful information to people. An honest leader is welcomed by all and sundry.

In order to develop your leadership makes a consistent effort to deal fairly, sincerely and genuinely in your personal relationship with people. Always keep your eyes open when moving to the next step in your life. **Each and every step in the ladder requires honest approach.** Therefore, keep climbing and forging ahead under the supervision of honesty.

Leadership development does not come overnight. It takes time and effort. Always accept and be opened to any change that life brings. Everything changes with the changing of time. Change is the law of nature. Your leadership is subject to constant change. A positive change in your own character brings honesty in you. **Always work hard to change for better!**

Whatever you do in life, it requires the blessing of honesty. Your approach and relationships with people become strong when you apply honesty. Nobody will accompany you towards your destiny. In order to reach your destiny safely, you need to have honesty in your character. Honesty will make you conscious of keeping yourself open to learn anything in your life. With honesty, you will realize although you have read or understood something, yet there are rooms for improvement.

On the road to leadership development, you need to re-vamp fairness and truthfulness. **Honesty is the magic behind all forms of successes in your life. Honesty demands humility and this is the theme of the next chapter.**

20

LEADERSHIP AND HUMILITY

Humility is one of the most important ingredients to leadership development. It is the ability to develop humbleness. Humility will protect you from falling prey to arrogance. It will help you to remain in balance, in your thought and judgment. **Humility opens the gate way to self-knowledge acquisition and change. This is possible through self-respect and respect of others. Self-knowledge will make you conscious that you are part and parcel of the wheel of life. The life of an individual, changes with the changing of times. Accepting change and keeping oneself in equilibrium in the unstable situation, make humility feasible.**

You should not attach to your duty. Perform all your duties for the sake of duties. This will relieve you from negative emotions.

Humility will keep you alert to incoming upheavals and will help you to deal with them with courage and self-commitment. Once you have developed humility, you will not be scared to venture into challenging situation. Humility makes your inner security possible. It makes you ready to face the challenges of life with a smile. **Developing humility indicates self-mastery.** It also shows that you have conquered arrogance. Humility will further help you to develop trust and self-confidence. When this happens, your subconscious mind starts to awaken your inner power and potential to face all types of eventualities. You will remain in self-control in a happy and unhappy situation. You will also realize an internal equilibrium and harmony. With humility, you will experience peace, joy and happiness in all your relationships.

Further, humility will enable you to examine your emotional blocks. To get rid of this, you will waste no time to deal with them. **Therefore, humility will make introspection possible. With this, you will develop self-esteem, self-control and inner stability.**

21

LEADERSHIP
AND COMPASSION

Compassion is another essential instrument for developing your leadership. Like humility, it awakens your respect for others. Compassion is the ability to incline to mercy, pity and sympathy to the weak entity.

Anybody who is suffering from physical or mental difficulty needs help. Never laugh at the sufferings of others. Whenever possible help all those who need support. **Compassion is applied to all plants, animals, human beings, living things and non living things. Help a needy and weak entity to stand on its own feet. Respect the air, water and light—the three great forces of life.** Encourage any needy individual to develop his or her inner power and potential.

Always perform your duty for the good of others. The world has set examples of compassionate people, Florence Nightingale, Mother Teresa and Gautama Buddha. Compassion will enable you to cast away negative thoughts from your mind. With compassion, you will develop the ability to perceive needs without judgment. It will also allow you to send support to the needy. **By seeing everybody with the eyes of respect, you purify your inner self.** Never promote yourself by taking advantage of the weak, innocent or poor. There are people in the world who are self-centered and always work for self-interest. **A life is worthy when it brings light in the lives of other.**

Nowadays, many people live close to one another in the same flat, house, locality or country, but in their social relationships, they are quite aloof. Living distance with one another creates the seed of arrogance, jealousy, hatred and ill-will. Many problems of relationships can be overcome by developing compassion.

With compassion, you will safely cross the ocean of life. Concentrate on the objectives set by you and work relentlessly to accomplish them with love, devotion, respect and sacrifice. You will create a conducive internal environment for the seed of compassion to germinate.

22

LEADERSHIP
AND SELF-CONTROL

Self-control is a powerful instrument for leadership development. Many people encounter failure in their lives owing to lack of self-control. Control is the ability to restrain from doing things that can bring negative results. Self-control is your power of controlling your emotions, behaviors and thoughts. It is one of the most important disciplines for the development of leadership. If the senses are not controlled, they behave like uncontrolled horses.

Not controlling the sense of taste, for example, can enable a person to eat food that is unhealthy. High level of oil, salt or sugar, leads to heart diseases, hypertension and diabetes. Most of the time, human beings perceive things outwardly using the sense organs of sight, touch, hearing, taste and feeling. Apart from this what is highly important is to perceive things inwardly. By activating the pituitary gland of your brain, you can have a good control over your senses. This structure of your brain is also called the master gland. Regular concentration through meditation activates it. Very often this structure has been referred to as the third eye. It is located in the middle of the forehead and in between the eyebrows. One of its responsibilities is to have a control over senses. Vibrations from the third eye influence the subconscious mind. When the third eye is activated, it leads to visualization and conceptualization.

Your subconscious mind has mastery over all your senses. Your most powerful self-controlling instrument is your subconscious mind. The register and carrier of the fruits of your action is your spirit. Your spirit is the master of your whole body. When your senses are under control, then you reach the goal of your life. Uncontrolled senses lead to pain, suffering and misery in life.

When the roots of a tree are strong and healthy, the tree thrives. The roots absorb water, nutrients and keep the tree anchored firmly in the ground. The roots are the important structures for the life of the tree. Similarly, your senses are connected by nerves from your brain. Impulses keep on moving to and fro from your brain each second. Some impulses are controlled by your subconscious mind, for example, heartbeat, breathing rate and internal digestion.

The very survival of your leadership lies on the self-control. True joy, happiness and peace originate from your subconscious mind. Your subconscious mind is your key to control all your senses. Empower it and see the wonders it brings to your leadership.

23

LEADERSHIP AND SELF-MOTIVE

A positive motive is a driving force which triggers your leadership development. It is a factor that induces you to act and drive towards your goal. Your positive thoughts, words and feelings, are the motivating machinery to keep you moving in life. A positive motive activates your imagination which leads to behavioral changes. Human behavior is associated with motivation. This is a process whereby a person's interest is stimulated, directed and maintained over a certain period of time. Therefore, motivation, demands a consistent activation of a person's behavior.

The quality of your work depends on your motivation. When you set a goal, a drive arises in your subconscious mind. Consequently, your subconscious mind releases energy to satisfy the drive. This drive is often called as a motive. It has a direct bearing on you behavior patterns. Behavior of an individual is influenced by factors such as self-esteem, personal identity, finance, competence, power, status and pride.

Developing self-motive requires self-discipline, self-commitment, positive attitude, self-confidence and self-patience as discussed in the previous chapters of this book. Your positive mental make-up plays a key role in the motivation phenomenon. Spend at least 30 minutes in silence every day. Send positive vibrations to your subconscious mind by thinking success, progress, happiness and peace. In all your actions, apply optimism. This is positive hope and confidence about the future. Here you need to be careful, do not dwell in the future. Detach yourself from the results of your action. Remember to live with the present. Leave your results and expectations in the hands of your subconscious mind. Do not bring any hurdle in your present moment.

Your subconscious mind will take up all your positive expectations and will process them positively. Never and never invite pessimism in your life. A pessimist person sees only a difficulty when an opportunity comes. A pessimist person always grumbles and invites trouble. The subconscious mind processes the negative energy generated by such a person. The outcome of a pessimist is often negative. Therefore, think positively, live positively and move positively in your life.

Water the garden of your subconscious mind with love, affection and devotion. Golden flowers from your subconscious mind will enlighten your leadership.

24

LEADERSHIP AND THE POWER OF FORGIVENESS

Forgiveness is a fundamental ingredient of leadership development. To forgive means to cease to feel angry. Forgiveness is, therefore, the act of forgiving. The power of forgiveness relates to your potential and ability to forgive others for a wrong thought, word or act. To apply the power of forgiveness in your life, you need to have honesty, courage, faith, self-control, self-discipline, inner power, righteousness and serenity. The act of forgiveness demands a strong control over your negative emotions. **Nobody is perfect in this world. Perfection lies only in God. An act is an event of the past. Digging and unearthing a past mistake in the present show human weakness. The past has gone. The present is the reality. If you have committed either a small or big negative act, do not bring mental torture. God forgives everybody who repents sincerely and faithfully for a negative act, then why you cannot forgive yourself? A negative act is committed because of ignorance or lack of control over your mind.**

Empower your subconscious mind, you will always think positively. **Remember that all your body cells change and are replaced by new ones. You have, therefore, changed physically, physiologically and psychologically. You are no longer the same person who committed either a small or big negative act. From now on, look at your life from a fresh perspective. Let by-gone be by-gone.** You need to release and free your subconscious mind from any block. A block occurs due to impurities accumulated in the pathway of your subconscious mind. **Never create tension and stress on your subconscious mind by inviting past errors.** Your subconscious mind is a very powerful instrument to clear and process negative emotions.

By forgiving someone for repenting his or her mistake, you do not become low in rank. On the contrary, you step ahead of others. It is important to note that by forgiving someone who has hurt you do not always imply that you intend to join him or her. Remember that you are entitled to your action only. Do not worry unnecessarily about the results of the act of forgiveness. Results of your act are not within your reach.

Also, you cannot enjoy the fruits of action perform by other people. A person has to confront the consequences of his or her action. The law of action says, as you sow, so shall you reap. Therefore, you should not worry about the action performed by other people. Always concentrate on the problem facing a person. Do not spend your energy criticizing a person who has committed an error. **Focus your attention on the problem itself instead of on the person. Never attack the person, but attack the problem.** A person commits an error or blunder because of his or her negative thoughts. Help such a person to develop a positive attitude to his or her life. A positive attitude towards life uproots and dissolves negative thoughts from the mind.

Remember that if someone repents faithfully for his or her error, God forgives such a person. God loves you. By repenting sincerely for your error, you are forgiven by God. Know for certain that once you are forgiven, all your sins are completely cleared. You become a righteous person again provided you sincerely, faithfully and trustfully admit for an error. According to the law of nature, you are forgiven hundreds of thousands of time. If you cut or burn your hand, your body reacts by forgiving you. It starts to replace your body cells, tissues and skin. If you generate positive thoughts, your subconscious mind brings back your vitality, happiness and peace.

One of the best ways to forgive is to sit silently and think positively on the person who hurts you. Say, I am fully forgiving you for whatever had happened in the past. The past has gone. Now I am completely free and absolutely free. I wish everybody happiness and peace. After forgiveness, you will feel lightness, freshness and vitality as if you have just taken a fresh bath.

Remember that nothing is bad or good, it is only thinking makes it so. Admit positively all your desires that nature has bestowed upon you. If anybody criticizes you then take the criticism as an opportunity to build up and correct any fault that you may have done. If you intentionally do not forgive, then you are bound by your own negative action. Once this happens you will have to reap the fruits of your own action. The power of forgiveness will help you move towards compassion and generosity. Compassion increases mercy and generosity will help you to look beyond the mistakes of others. **Forgiveness is to give joy, happiness, peace, wisdom and blessings to others. A life lived for the good of others, is a good life.**

25

LEADERSHIP AND ACCEPTANCE

Acceptance is an important constituent of leadership development. Accepting yourself the way you are, helps to create an inner force. You are the only one to generate your own inner force. Everybody possesses tremendous potential to face any situation in life. This potential comes from within oneself. Always accept that you have all the ingredients required for leadership development. Acceptance is your ability to affirm and approve your inner potential. Acceptance is developed by increasing your tolerance level. Tolerance is the capacity to face negative emotions. An increase in your tolerance level helps to overcome negative emotions. Tolerance develops from your compassion. It gives you the ability to accept people from all walks of life. Through tolerance, you grow stronger and healthier. By constantly feeding your subconscious mind with positive thoughts, the negative emotions die.

Accepting your inner potential goes a long way towards knowing your own identity. Your identity is revealed by the qualities you possess. Your individuality and leadership are special attributes. It is by accepting, you are able to experience your own attributes. Your individuality is distinct from others. You are a unique creation in this world.

Recognize yourself by accepting this truth and reality. Cultivate the habit of accepting yourself by regularly sending positive thoughts to your subconscious mind. Your positive thoughts generate positive vibrations. Avoid any negative thought on you, for example, thinking weak. **Remember strength is life and weakness is death.** Accepting yourself does not mean that others are inferior and you are superior. It is far from any arrogance. Always be yourself in all situations. You are special, unique, dynamic and powerful. This is your reality. Cast off any unhealthy feeling towards you. You are capable of constructing your own destiny. By accepting yourself, you will change everything that is negative into positive. Look at yourself in the mirror and accept yourself. Constantly build up your inner power and potential. Your leadership will glow and success will emerge in all your undertakings.

Your subconscious mind plays a vital role in shaping your leadership. The first and foremost thing is to generate positive thoughts. This activates your subconscious mind. Once this has occurred, positive vibrations from your subconscious mind, starts to flower your leadership.

26

LEADERSHIP
AND RESPONSIBILITY

Responsibility is another very important constituent of leadership development. Responsibility is the ability to act independently. Nobody can take responsibility of your actions. The law of action says, as you sow, so shall you reap. Also, you cannot escape from the fruits of your actions. The rewards or fruits of your action can be juicy or spicy. Thus, you are the only one responsible for the results of your action.

By responsibility, I mean that you are liable to account for your action. Your thoughts, decisions or feelings, are associated with your act. An idea germinates in your mind. Then you put the idea into action. The action brings the fruit of your labor. In the whole process, your responsibility lies. People can only give advice on a course of action, but the action is to be performed by you. Once you do the action, you become responsible for your action.

There are some people who blame others for their own wrong actions. Inflicting blame on others for your action is a sign of weakness. You must learn to stand on your own feet by taking full responsibility. Responsibility will enable you to thread on the righteous path. By assuming personal responsibility, you will develop your character, self-confidence and self-reliance. Always learn to depend on yourself. Believe in your own strength and power.

Develop your personal responsibility by thinking positively. By sitting in silence for at least 30 minutes daily, you cultivate inner power. By doing so, you become a dynamo of energy. Regular meditation will improve your self-confidence and self-control ability. Your role in life is unique and a special one. Therefore, know your importance by taking personal responsibility in all your undertakings. Each time you will go through a responsibility, you will feel that you have grown and have become strong in your life. This will stimulate your subconscious mind to release positive vibrations.

27

LEADERSHIP AND THE POWER OF CONCENTRATION

Concentration is the key to leadership development. Your clear thinking and intellectual ability, will lead you towards success in your life. The rays of your mind are scattered in various directions like that of the sun's rays. When the sun's rays are concentrated through a glass lens, power is generated. This has the ability to set fire. The world is full of knowledge. It is by the power of concentration that the knowledge of the world is revealed. All discoveries and inventions in this world have been made by the concentrated minds of the scientists.

Concentration is your ability to focus attention on one point. Once you have developed this ability, the power of our subconscious mind increases. With a concentrated mind, you are able to knock and open the secrets of knowledge. The power of your subconscious mind is beyond the limit. Everything is possible in this world for a concentrated mind. The treasure house of knowledge is opened by the power of your concentrated mind. In order to increase the power of concentration, you need to generate positive thoughts constantly.

Many people feel miserable and frustrated because of their inabilities to have a control on their minds. **Lack of concentration is the root cause of failure in life.** A person whose mind is unstable moves aimlessly in his or her life. When you set a clear cut goal in your life, your subconscious mind starts to accumulate power. It concentrates your attention on the goal. Your subconscious mind is your greatest weapon to make success possible in all your undertakings. Know for certain that you have the ability and potential to shape your own destiny in this world. Your success is enclosed in your subconscious mind. Learn to give it a knock and blow. Once it is opened, strength and power will emerge in you.

One of the ways to develop concentration is by regular meditation. This helps to attain steady and concentrated mind. Your mind needs to be fixed on your inner self. It needs to be in perfect self-control. To attain an ideal state of mind, you need to practice meditation regularly.

Meditation will help you to accumulate power in silence. A simple way to do this is to sit comfortably with legs crossed and fingers interlocked. This creates an energy field within you. Gently close your eyes and observe your breath. Your breathing should be natural. You will feel internal silence submerging you. You will feel isolation and calmness.

Let yourself drown in this silence. When any thought emerges in your mind, do not flow it. Just observe that thought like a spectator. The length between two thoughts will enlarge. Thought is an obstacle on the path to meditation. It is like a wave in pond. The presence of waves in the water will prevent you to see at the bottom of the pond. In the absence of the waves, you will be able to observe clearly living creatures in the pond. In the same manner, do not germinate thoughts in your mind. If any thought comes, just observe it. Do not follow such a thought. Soon, it will die. When your mind is clear and calm, you are ready for an internal voyage.

By using your imagination reach your toes. Imagine your body is hanging like a kite on a hill. Little by little move upward through your heels, knees and reach the first energy center. You have seven major energy centers and thousands of minor centers called *chakra*. Continue to ascend and imagine that all parts of your body that are being left are lifeless.

Move up through each energy center from the base of your spine, sacrum, navel, heart, neck, forehead and crown. After reaching the crown '*chakra*', use the same technique to return to your initial position. Move slowly and gently down each '*chakra*'. After reaching your toes, rub your eyes with both hands before opening them. Practice this simple meditation daily for at least 45 minutes. If you want to know more about meditation, please read my books: **'Your window to silence and peace'** and **'Blown by the wind of true peace and happiness through yogic meditation'**. Meditation will enable you to become a dynamo of energy and power.

Therefore, concentration is vital for developing leadership. It has the power to unlock the hidden knowledge of the world. This is the theme of the next chapter.

28

LEADERSHIP AND SELF-KNOWLEDGE

Self-knowledge is an essential constituent of leadership development. The knowledge of the world originates from the human mind. The world is ready to reveal its secrets provided that you have the necessary skill to open the treasure house of knowledge. All inventions and discoveries have come from the power of mind. Hundreds of thousands of people's lives have been improved by knowledge.

The knowledge comes from the awareness or familiarity gained by experience. Therefore, the knowledge is not necessarily gained by going to school, college or university. There are many people who have gained knowledge by their own experience in their lives. Some have never gone to school, but they have been very successful in gaining knowledge in their lives. Henry Ford had very little schooling, yet he made tremendous progress in his life. He succeeded in his business by putting people on wheels. Robert Burns lived in absolute poverty and did not attend schooling, yet he became a renowned man for his poetry.

Milton was blind and Beethoven suffered from deafness, yet both imprinted their names in history.

The world is bounded with examples of people who have gained knowledge by their own. Knowledge of life is gained from the home, society, country, world and universe. Knowledge is obtained by studying different sciences, art, philosophy and humanities. By reading good books, one gets knowledge. Books are essential instruments of wisdom's treasure. But self-knowledge comes from direct experience of life. Your subconscious mind has the power to unravel the celestial knowledge. This knowledge is gained through deep concentration. It is the most powerful one. It reveals the very existence of your life. Self-knowledge cannot be obtained by reading books or listening to lectures, but by direct revelation of the self. Self-knowledge of this nature is received by all those people who are receptive.

One of the goals of your life is to have self-knowledge. Remember a little or inadequate knowledge is dangerous. People who have a little knowledge on a subject matter develop arrogance. **A person who is well versed in knowledge has a balance mind and intellect. Such a person never criticizes other people's opinion, but respect their views.**

29

LEADERSHIP AND ENTHUSIASM

Enthusiasm is an essential ingredient for leadership development. All great discoveries and inventions in life have been achieved by enthusiasm. Enthusiasm will make you active, energetic and powerful. It creates a strong will power and interest in a person. Learn to listen to your inner voice, awaken your dormant spirit and see the wonders that you can bring to the world. Enthusiasm is a heavenly given gift to you. Use this inner power to enlighten your leadership.

Develop your enthusiasm through inspiration from positive feelings and emotions. Enthusiasm is triggered by strong feeling of interest, excitement, eagerness and zeal. Enthusiasm will make all your actions enjoyable and exciting. A strong positive approach to all your understandings will make your life thrilling and joyful. Enthusiasm is the magic power generated by your subconscious mind. A person who is enthusiastic, always works with contentment on any difficult assignment.

Nothing is impossible for an enthusiastic person. In deep silence, you will be able to activate the release of the power of enthusiasm. In tranquility, your subconscious mind activates your sense of hearing, touch, feeling, taste and sight. Impulses from your sense organs make you enthusiastic. Enthusiasm makes you compassionate, self-confident, self-discipline and self-motivated. It is a priceless component of your leadership. If you are an enthusiastic person, then you are always welcomed by everybody. An enthusiastic person brings light in the life of others. Such a person always glows with cheer, high spirits, drives and positive attitude. Enthusiasm will keep you always moving ahead in life.

Develop enthusiasm by generating positive thoughts. Every morning spend at least 15 minutes thinking good things about you and others. Fill your mind with positive sayings and words. Develop positive feelings about nature. Meditate at least 30 minutes daily. Ask your higher Being to guide you in all your undertakings. **Develop complete trust, faith and confidence in you. Do physical exercise regularly and live with a full heart every second of your life.**

30

LEADERSHIP AND PERSONALITY

Personality is the cornerstone of leadership development. It is the distinctive features or qualities that you possess. A well-developed personality will keep you progressing in your life. The term personality relates to your outer and inner aspects of your individuality. Your physical appearance, voice, dress and manners constitute the external aspects of your personality. On the other hand, the inner lights of your personality relate to, for example, respect, determination, humility, honesty, faith, knowledge, confidence, compassion, discipline, enthusiasm, courage, patience, commitment, positive manners and self-control.

Your personality needs to be constantly re-polished, re-visited and re-engineered in the changing environment of your life. The radiance of your magnetic personality will continue to glisten your leadership if you apply the gems contained in this book. You will always be attracted by people and swarmed around like honey bees to a flower. People will listen you with rapt attention and you will spark fine flame of wisdom wherever you will go. Personality is not totally a divine given gift, but it depends largely on how you make it. Here are some of ways to develop personality.

- Constantly improve your thoughts, emotions and feelings. Always thrive to flourish positive thoughts, good feelings and positive emotions.

- Always keep a good company. Choose your company with great care and attention. Always mix with people who have positive attitude and wisdom. Positive associations with people will enhance your personality development through vision, positive emotions and feelings.

- A good environment has a strong impact on your personality development. Maintain your physical, biological and psycho-social environment. A positive environment influences self-image development and personality.

- Never put any blame on other people. Take full responsibility of your actions.

- Do not inflate a small problem. Also, do not make a huge mountain out of a mole hills. Always reduce the size of a problem by cutting it into pieces as explained earlier in this book. Never run away from your problems. It is not by running away, but by facing boldly any problem you will become victorious in life. Deal with one problem at a time. With firm confidence and faith you will be able to handle any problem of your life.

- Do not criticize other people unnecessarily. Any constructive criticism must be done with respect, love, affection and positive desire to improve any individual. Encourage and learn to appreciate the performance of others.

- Avoid dwelling under strain of idealism and perfectionism. Do not hope to get perfection in all actions. It is vital to understand that real perfection lies only in God. At times, mistakes do happen. Learn to grow from your own mistakes as they are life-lessons in wisdom. Take immediate action to rectify any mistake. A stitch in time saves nine.

- Be humble in your approach. Arrogance leads to the downfall of mankind. So, do not show off your material position such as wealth, name, power and fame to other people.

- Learn to let go and give up past events. Do not awaken dead and buried things of the past. Also, do not worry unnecessarily about the future events. Leave fully on the present moment of your life.

- Learn to acknowledge your weaknesses and take immediate action to overcome them. Be true to yourself. This will help to bring internal harmony in you.

- Have compassion to the needs of others. Wherever possible provide assistance to the needy.

- Improve and develop your imagination. It is your blueprint for your personality development.

- Do not deceive your own potential. Be honest and considerate to your actions.

- Cultivate positive habits. This will help you to develop harmonious relationship with people.

- Do not copy the behaviors of others. Be yourself in all circumstances. Never stop growing in the pathway to personality development.

By applying constantly the above mentioned tips you will be able to cast away impurities and doubts. What will then remain is a pure and shinning outgoing personality filled with wisdom and goodness.

31

LEADERSHIP AND VISION

Leadership is incomplete without a clear cut vision. An effective leader has a crystal clear vision of the eventual goal he or she wishes to attain. Without a vision you will encounter utter failure in your life. Nurture your vision through your senses. Energize your vision by setting specific goals which are realizable. By writing down your goals in clear terms, set a clear plan of action in order to execute it. Your goals are the guiding light of your vision. It is the stepping-stone to reach your destination safe and sound. The pathways of leaders are not always smooth, but paved with difficulties and obstacles at times. After defining your vision for yourself, set realistic goals to attain. By developing a goal-oriented habit, you will consolidate your leadership potential.

There are generally three major types of goals, short-term, medium-term and long-term. Short-term goals represent immediate action. It is accomplished quickly with effort and good plan. A medium-term goal very often requires several steps and planning. It represents midrange between short-term and long-term goals. Such a goal requires consistent effort for its accomplishment. As far as long-term goal is concerned, it is future directed for a longer period of time. It is related to a person's life long career or profession.

You can use the following tips to establish realistic goals. Each goal will help you to realize your vision as a leader.

- Write down your goals on a paper. Be committed to accomplish your goals. It is advisable to share your goals with experienced people. Seek assistance and obtain help from knowledgeable people.

- Set realistic, worthwhile and attainable goals.

- Your goals should be flexible and subject to changes in the environment.

- Define your goals in specific, concrete and measurable terms.

- Set a good plan to attain your goals.

- Check and validate your goals constantly.

- Evaluate the outcome of your goals.

A vision guides a leader to move courageously in the mighty ocean like a ship's compass. It gives a proper direction and orientation towards your journey. Thus, a clear vision helps a leader to crystallize precisely what he or she wishes to attain.

32

LEADERSHIP
AND IMAGINATION

Imagination is one of the important features of leadership development. The creative faculty of an individual enables him or her to convert wind into a source of light and energy. Imagination of a leader involves the constructive intellectual grouping of knowledge into new, rational and original form. Great leaders of the world such as Bill Gates, Richard Branson, Barack Obama, Warren Buffet and Amancio Ortega have always used imagination in their leadership endeavor. Albert Einstein and Larry Elison attained great height in their lives by using imagination in their inventions and discoveries. Imagination stimulates progress and advancement in the world. A leader can use imagination synthetically or creatively. Synthetic imagination involves examination of concepts, facts or ideas whereas creative imagination covers the areas of artists, musicians, writers, politics, economics and scientists. Leaders like Rabindranath Tagore and Leonardo da Vinci had produced immortal creative works through their imaginations.

As a leader use your imagination to connect your own consciousness with that of universal consciousness. By doing so, you will be able to change the formless energy of the universal mind into a constructive form in your own mind. One of the ways to empower your imagination is to bring yourself to alpha state by stilling your mind through meditation as explained earlier in this book. Learn to relax your mental turmoil and raise the power of your imagination as advised below.

- Bring inner peace through regular meditation.

- Stimulate your mental faculty by reading intensively.

- Form a clear pathway to achieve your goals.

- Empower your imagination by regular practice. Use meditative techniques for bringing inner peace.

- Learn to develop the power of concentration as explained in this book.

- Have a perfect control over your emotions and moods.

- Have faith in your own potential.

- Be innovative and creative in your ideas.

- Develop positive habits for imagination.

- Use your subconscious mind regularly in your day to day activities.

Remember that your power of imagination will go a long way towards your leadership development. It is an effective tool for your progress and advancement in life.

33

LEADERSHIP AND AMBITION

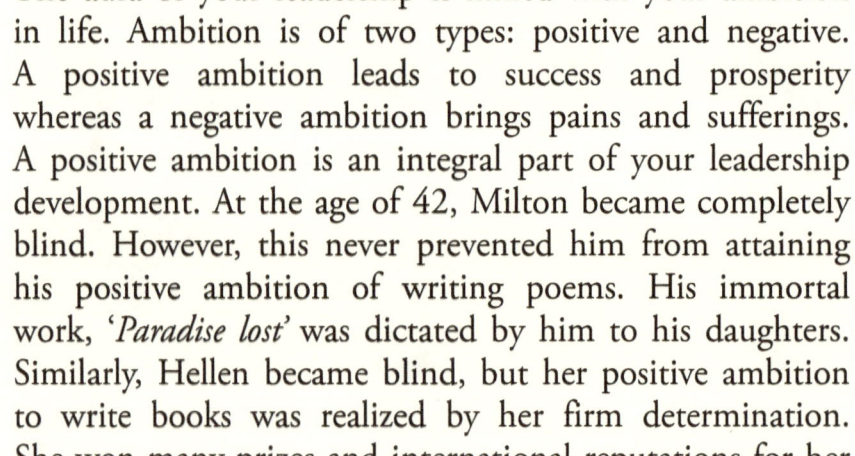

The aura of your leadership is linked with your ambition in life. Ambition is of two types: positive and negative. A positive ambition leads to success and prosperity whereas a negative ambition brings pains and sufferings. A positive ambition is an integral part of your leadership development. At the age of 42, Milton became completely blind. However, this never prevented him from attaining his positive ambition of writing poems. His immortal work, 'Paradise lost' was dictated by him to his daughters. Similarly, Hellen became blind, but her positive ambition to write books was realized by her firm determination. She won many prizes and international reputations for her writings. At no point in time, Lincoln and Tagore gave up their positive ambitions when faced with great difficulties in their lives. They moved ahead peacefully through their difficulties to attain their positive ambitions.

Germinate the seed of your positive ambition with love and devotion. Nurture and protect it from harsh weather conditions. Stick to it until you are crowned with success.

A leader without a positive ambition is like a rudderless ship sailing in the mighty rough ocean without a proposed destination. Such a leader tosses and drifts aimlessly by the passing waves. A positive ambition is vital for leadership development. It provides the necessary back up and impulse for moving on the pathway of success.

Great leaders like Copernicus, Newton, Galileo and Einstein worked relentlessly towards their goals. They changed the destiny of the world by their inventions and discoveries. The world is full of examples of leaders who made progress in their lives from scratch. Nobody could have imagined Abraham Lincoln who lived in a shabby cabin without money to finance his education would be the President of America one day? History shows that leaders who were underprivileged in their early lives made tremendous progress through hard and relentless effort.

Therefore, stick to your positive ambition and continue to push up the ladder of advancement and progress. Remember, great souls always have positive ambitions in their lives.

34

LEADERSHIP AND FAILURE

Your road to leadership development is at times paved with obstacles and difficulties. The leader Alexandra De Seversky faced many failures during World War I, before flying more than fifty times to Russia with one leg. Guglielmo Marconi lost one of his eyes, before inventing radio. Likewise, John Logie Baird faced several failures, before inventing television. Similarly, Richard Nixon like Abraham Lincoln failed many times, before succeeding in Presidential elections.

The life of leaders is a mixture of successes and failures. Effective leaders struggle ceaselessly against failures. Learn to change failure into success. Failures are the pillars to success in the lives of leaders. Life has both ups and downs. Dark clouds never stay eternally in the sky. After darkness, daylight comes. So, continue to develop your leadership despite hurdles on your way. Remember that any farmer, before reaping a bumper harvest has to face initially hazards of weather conditions and pests. Success in leadership development involves taking risks. Failures in a person's life judge the value of courage, patience, determination, faith, discipline and commitment.

Every day is a fresh day. Always remember that yesterday has gone. Do not worry unnecessarily about past failures. If any mistake has been the root cause of your failure, then work hard to rectify the mistake. Remember that great leaders of the world had to face failures in their early lives. They, too, had to face mistakes done by them. There is no human being in this world, who had not faced failures or had done mistakes in his or her life. However, intelligent an individual may be, he or she is liable to mistake or failure. Great leaders of the world had attained greatness through relentless efforts by moving boldly against failures. Do not scold at a person who had done a mistake. It will shatter his or her confidence.

As an effective leader do not attack the person, but attack the mistake. Concentrate on how to attack and tackle a mistake instead of the person who has done the mistake. Mistakes need to be acknowledged and corrected immediately. If you recognize your own mistakes and failures, you are then one step ahead in the process of removing them. Do some self-introspection and work hard to improve your leadership. Brooding over past mistakes cripples positive thoughts and it leads to tension. Also, do not shift responsibility on other people for your own mistakes.

Leadership development involves learning how to take all the jerks and jolts to your stride. Mistakes and failure are the stepping-stone to leadership development. They may appear unpleasant to leaders, but in reality, they are a blessing in disguise. You should never dread mistakes or failure on your pathway to leadership development and excellence. Thus, at times, people have to face the sweat of mistakes and failures, before reaping a bumper harvest of leadership.

35

LEADERSHIP AND CRITICISM

In the process of your leadership development, you may face critics from others. A constructive criticism helps a leader to improve his leadership whereas a negative criticism hurts a leader. Criticism is the part and parcel of leadership development. The world provides many examples of great leaders whose achievements in leadership were often laughed at the beginning. Abraham Lincoln was severely criticized during the American Civil War. At no point in time, he showed anger when he was criticized by his own people. He kept his mind peaceful. George Washington was declared as a hypocrite and press cartoon showed him on a guillotine ready to chop his head with a knife. Despite severe criticism, he never stopped his struggle on the pathway to liberate America.

Great leaders like Mahatma Gandhi and Margaret Thatcher had to face tremendous criticism in their attempts to bring socio-political change in their countries. Edward Jenner was severely criticized for his contribution in the field of medicine. Despite this, he continued to forge ahead and eventually he was crowned with success by discovering vaccine against smallpox.

Galileo is another example of scientist who had to encounter tremendous criticism from his adversaries. Some individuals threw mud on his research and discovery. But, he changed all criticisms inflicted on him into constructive ones. He took them as a challenge to face the battle of life. Galileo kept all his critics at bay and he just concentrated on how to turn them into positive ones.

Remember that great leaders had always encountered hostility in their campaign against, socio-political upliftment. Such leaders had displayed commitment, determination, patience, and courage in their endeavor to face monstrous criticism.

Recently I won the first prize in a public debate. I was congratulated by friends for my excellence performance. Media did a positive propaganda. The very next day my adversaries made negative critics on my performance. I kept their critics at a distance by turning them. into positive ones. I prevented the negative criticism to touch me. I remain neutral and took all critics positively. Remember, you may be garlanded with happiness for your success today, people around you may throw mud and you may face critics tomorrow. Therefore, never be carried away with negative criticism of others. Look at any negative criticism with a proper spirit. Keep your emotions under perfect control by empowering your subconscious mind as explained earlier in this book.

36

LEADERSHIP AND EMOTIONS

Emotions are intertwined with leadership development. There are two types of emotions: good and bad. A good emotion makes you attractive and it increases your joy. On the other hand, a bad emotion like fear, jealousy, greed, worry, stress, hatred, tension and anger create upheavals. In the process of leadership development, you must discard negative emotions. **An effective leader, never allows himself or herself to be carried away by any emotion. He or she remains neutral in all circumstances. If you are drifted by emotions by facing a given situation then this shows your weakness.**

By remaining peaceful and tranquil, the gate of your subconscious mind opens. This allows the generation of positive thoughts. A negative emotion develops owing to a lack of balanced mind and intellect. Great leaders of the world have always controlled their emotions in all environments. In the section below, I have given some advices on how to overcome your negative emotions.

- Cultivate and develop self-confidence, trust, faith, discipline, compassion, self-commitment, self-determination and detachment!

- Remember that all negative emotions are removable.

- Write down the negative emotion on a paper. Always aim at reducing the size of a negative emotion.

- Do not allow yourself to be attached with your negative emotion.

- Use your subconscious mind to empower your approach in dealing with your negative emotions.

- Use a heading and jot down all the possible ways to tackle your negative emotions.

- Imagine your success in this endeavor all the times.

- At no point in time, you should react to any negative emotion. Simply, focus your attention on how to overcome your negative emotions.

- Remember to remain detach with your negative emotions.

- Now, use another heading how you will dissolve all the points you have listed. Write constructively and firmly on how you want to dissolve each of your negative emotion. Observe your inner potential emerging during this operation. You will attain success in overcoming all your negative emotions by this approach.

Your road to leadership development is often paved with emotions that can increase your happiness or kill your incentive. Therefore, the choice is yours. By using the above mentioned advices and the guidelines given in the different sections of this book, you will certainly attain success in leadership development.

37

LEADERSHIP AND TOLERANCE

Tolerance is one of the essential aspects of leadership development. Tolerance relates to the ability to tolerate a demanding situation or condition. Great leaders have high tolerance level for emotional imbalance or changing circumstance in their pathways to their goals realization. A high tolerance level is a great virtue possessed by a leader.

Develop your tolerance level by empowering your subconscious mind. If anyone inflicts insults, harsh words or critics on you then do not admit them. Always look at these negations from a distance. You should remain neutral and unaffected by unexpected negative circumstances. A leader, who possesses a high tolerance level, achieves great height in his or her life by crossing all hurdles and barriers.

Learn the ability to forget and forgive the misdoings of others. Keep your subconscious mind empty. Do not allow the accumulation of negative emotions in your subconscious mind. Your subconscious mind possesses tremendous power to increase your tolerance level. It stores a huge amount of permanent memory. Regularly feed your subconscious mind with positive thoughts. Replace any accumulation of negative emotion such as revenge, jealousy, fear, anger and hatred with positive emotion such as love, devotion and affection.

Control your reactions to the changing environment. Detach yourself from worldly things and conditions. A strong inner willpower will help you to develop a higher tolerance level in turbulent circumstances.

Your power of leadership is developed through high tolerance level. Great leaders do not lose their temper with adverse reactions or circumstances. During the presidential campaign, the late American President Cleveland was severely ostracized by a certain section of the American society. After being elected, people expected him to show negative emotions during the inaugural ceremony at Washington, but he kept himself cool and peaceful. This showed his high tolerance level in extremely demanding situation.

Therefore, learn to develop this highest virtue by being tolerant to the defects and shortcomings of other people. Your high tolerance level will help you to develop a strong leadership.

38

LEADERSHIP AND PERSITENCE

One of the most powerful components of leadership development is persistence. Consistent and sustained effort will make success achievable in your life. Your inner drive and willpower will enable you to move towards your objectives. Persistence is the continued action to accomplish something. A lack of persistence leads to failure in life. Many people after starting something they give up later. By applying persistence in your endeavor, you will assure your own success. Continue to move firmly and obstinately towards your goals.

Christopher Columbus had to move persistently forward despite great hurdles and barriers on his efforts, before discovering America in 1492. Henry Ford, is another example, of the value of persistence. Henry Ford had to face great barriers and difficulties in his business. Despite this, he never gave up. His persistent character crowned him with success. If today, I have been able to write this book, it is because of persistence. At no moment in my life, I have given up in my endeavor. Despite the failure in my examination and barriers in my early life, I persistently forged to arrive where I am currently standing.

Nothing great has ever been achieved without persistent effort. **If you look at an ant, you will learn the lesson of industry. An ant never stops moving if you block its way. It changes its direction and keeps on moving persistently towards its goal. A honey bee is a good example of persistence. It keeps on moving persistently from flower to flower in order to collect nectar.** All inventions and discoveries are products of sustained effort. Persistence is developed through self-discipline, self-control, self-patience, self-commitment and self-motive.

Develop persistence in your character and approach. Be persistent in all your endeavors. Empower your subconscious mind with positive thoughts. Learn to increase your power of concentration as explained in this book. Constantly make an effort to move ahead in your life by concentrating on your work.

Never criticize or involve in profitless talks, just work selflessly and confidently. Success will attain your footsteps. **Persistence is your weapon to develop a strong leadership. To develop persistence ensures that you have a clear cut goal, strong desire, knowledge, distinct plan of action and strong willpower.** Work daily on your personal qualities. You are a strong, courageous and enthusiastic person. Remember that behind your achievement and success in life there is always the power of persistence.

39

CONCLUSION

This book, '*Modern leadership development and excellence*', unravels the secret to your leadership development and excellence. It contains the discoveries of leadership development and excellence. This book is a masterpiece written by the author, Dr.S.K.Babooa, exclusively for you. By holding this book in your hands, take a firm decision now to look at your life with fresh eyes. You are a treasure house of power. This book has discussed the vital gems of leadership such as **the dormant power of your mind, positive attitude, faith, self-confidence, fearlessness, courage, self-determination, serenity, self-sacrifice, detachment, self-commitment, self-discipline, self-patience, righteousness, character, positive manner, honesty, humility, compassion, self-control and self-motive. It has also illustrated the backbone of leadership like the power of forgiveness, acceptance, responsibility, power of concentration, self-knowledge, enthusiasm personality, vision, imagination, ambition, failure, criticism, emotions tolerance and persistence.**

Your real-nature of leadership emerges from the manifestation of these gems. Today, the world needs you as a model of leadership excellence. To attain this, the book highlights the importance of casting away the veil that is hiding your leadership. The author, Dr. S.K.Babooa has presented in this book his own discovery on leadership by working with people in different walks of life for the last seventeen years. This is a life transforming book towards leadership excellence. The book says . . . *'Dwell fully in the present moment by opening a new chapter of this book in your life'*. **This book is a masterpiece for opening your doorway to leadership development and excellence**.

www.ingramcontent.com/pod-product-compliance
Lightning Source LLC
Chambersburg PA
CBHW020533290526
45786CB00002B/864